JAMESTOWN EDUCATION

TIMED READINGS

Third Edition

Fifty 400-Word Passages
with Questions for
Building Reading Speed

BOOK FOUR

Edward Spargo

Mc Graw Hill **Glencoe McGraw-Hill**

New York, New York   Columbus, Ohio   Chicago, Illinois   Peoria, Illinois   Woodland Hills, California

JAMESTOWN 🚢 EDUCATION

Titles in This Series
Timed Readings, Third Edition
Timed Readings in Literature

Teaching Notes are available for this text and
will be sent to the instructor. Please write on
school stationery; tell us what grade
you teach and identify the text.

Glencoe/McGraw-Hill 🖉

*A Division of The **McGraw·Hill** Companies*

Timed Readings, Third Edition
Book Four

Cover and text design: Deborah Hulsey Christie

ISBN: 0-89061-506-3

Send all queries:
Glencoe/McGraw-Hill
8787 Orion Place
Columbus, OH 43240-4027

22 23 24 ROV 15 14 13 12 11

Contents

Introduction to the Student

These *Timed Readings* are designed to help you become a faster and better reader. As you progress through the book, you will find yourself growing in reading speed and comprehension. You will be challenged to increase your reading rate while maintaining a high level of comprehension.

Reading, like most things, improves with practice. If you practice improving your reading speed, you will improve. As you will see, the rewards of improved reading speed will be well worth your time and effort.

Why Read Faster?

The quick and simple answer is that faster readers are better readers. Does this statement surprise you? You might think that fast readers would miss something and their comprehension might suffer. This is not true, for two reasons:

1. **Faster readers comprehend faster.** When you read faster, the writer's message is coming to you faster and makes sense sooner. Ideas are interconnected. The writer's thoughts are all tied together, each one leading to the next. The more quickly you can see how ideas are related to each other, the more quickly you can comprehend the meaning of what you are reading.

2. **Faster readers concentrate better.** Concentration is essential for comprehension. If your mind is wandering you can't understand what you are reading. A lack of concentration causes you to re-read, sometimes over and over, in order to comprehend. Faster readers concentrate better because there's less time for distractions to interfere. Comprehension, in turn, contributes to concentration. If you are concentrating and comprehending, you will not become distracted.

Want to Read More?

Do you wish that you could read more? (or, at least, would you like to do your required reading in less time?) Faster reading will help.

The illustration on the next page shows the number of books someone might read over a period of ten years. Let's see what faster reading could do for you. Look at the stack of books read by a slow reader and the stack

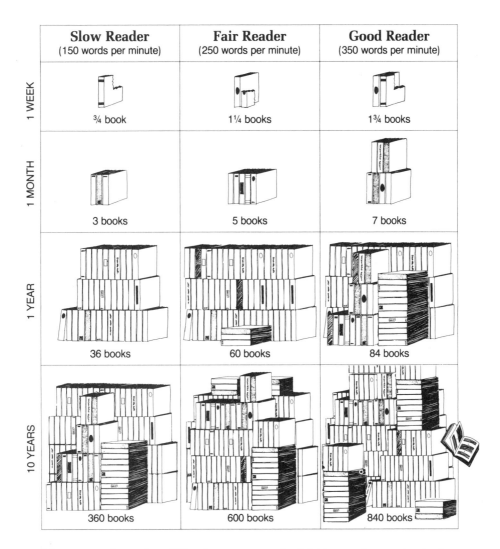

	Slow Reader (150 words per minute)	Fair Reader (250 words per minute)	Good Reader (350 words per minute)
1 WEEK	¾ book	1¼ books	1¾ books
1 MONTH	3 books	5 books	7 books
1 YEAR	36 books	60 books	84 books
10 YEARS	360 books	600 books	840 books

read by a good reader. (We show a speed of 350 words a minute for our "good" reader, but many fast readers can more than double that speed.) Let's say, however, that you are now reading at a rate of 150 words a minute. The illustration shows you reading 36 books a year. By increasing your reading speed to 250 words a minute, you could increase the number of books to 60 a year.

We have arrived at these numbers by assuming that the readers in our illustration read for one hour a day, six days a week, and that an average book is about 72,000 words long. Many people do not read that much, but they might if they could learn to read better and faster.

Faster reading doesn't *take* time, it *saves* time!

How to Use This Book

1 Learn the Four Steps Study and learn the four steps to follow to become a better and faster reader. The steps are covered on pages 9, 10, 11, and 12.

2 Preview Turn to the selection you are going to read and wait for the instructor's signal to preview. Your instructor will allow 30 seconds for previewing.

3 Begin reading When your instructor gives you the signal, begin reading. Read at a slightly faster-than-normal speed. Read well enough so that you will be able to answer questions about what you have read.

7 Fill in the progress graph Enter your score and plot your reading time on the graph on page 118 or 119. The right-hand side of the graph shows your words-per-minute reading speed. Write this number at the bottom of the page on the line labeled *Words per Minute.*

4 Record your time

When you finish reading, look at the blackboard and note your reading time. Your reading time will be the lowest time remaining on the board, or the next number to be erased. Write this time at the bottom of the page on the line labeled *Reading Time*.

5 Answer the questions

Answer the ten questions on the next page. There are five fact questions and five thought questions. Pick the *best* answer to each question and put an x in the box beside it.

6 Correct your answers

Using the Answer Key on pages 116 and 117, correct your work. Circle your wrong answers and put an x in the box you should have marked. Score 10 points for each correct answer. Write your score at the bottom of the page on the line labeled *Comprehension Score*.

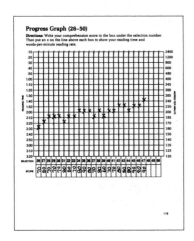

Instructions for the Pacing Drills

From time to time your instructor may wish to conduct pacing drills using *Timed Readings*. For this work you need to use the Pacing Dots printed in the margins of your book pages. The dots will help you regulate your reading speed to match the pace set by your instructor or announced on the reading cassette tape.

Pacing Dots

You will be reading at the correct pace if you are at the dot when your instructor says "Mark" or when you hear a tone on the tape. If you are ahead of the pace, read a little more slowly; if you are behind the pace, increase your reading speed. Try to match the pace exactly.

Follow these steps.

Step 1: Record the pace. At the bottom of the page, write on the line labeled *Words per Minute* the rate announced by the instructor or by the speaker on the tape.

Step 2: Begin reading. Wait for the signal to begin reading. Read at a slightly faster-than-normal speed. You will not know how on-target your pace is until you hear your instructor say "Mark" or until you hear the first tone on the tape. After a little practice you will be able to select an appropriate starting speed most of the time.

Step 3: Adjust your pace. As you read, try to match the pace set by the instructor or the tape. Read more slowly or more quickly as necessary. You should be reading the line beside the dot when you hear the pacing signal. The pacing sounds may distract you at first. Don't worry about it. Keep reading and your concentration will return.

Step 4: Stop and answer questions. Stop reading when you are told to, even if you have not finished the selection. Answer the questions right away. Correct your work and record your score on the line *Comprehension Score*. Strive to maintain 80 percent comprehension on each drill as you gradually increase your pace.

Step 5: Fill in the pacing graph. Transfer your words-per-minute rate to the box labeled *Pace* on the pacing graph on page 120. Then plot your comprehension score on the line above the box.

These pacing drills are designed to help you become a more flexible reader. They encourage you to "break out" of a pattern of reading everything at the same speed.

The drills help in other ways, too. Sometimes in a reading program you reach a certain level and bog down. You don't seem able to move on and progress. The pacing drills will help you to work your way out of such slumps and get your reading program moving again.

Steps to Faster Reading

STEP 1: PREVIEW

When you read, do you start in with the first word, or do you look over the whole selection for a moment? Good readers preview the selection first—this helps to make them good, and fast, readers.

1. Read the Title. The first thing to do when previewing is to read the title of the selection. Titles are designed not only to announce the subject, but also to make the reader think. What can you learn from the title? What thoughts does it bring to mind? What do you already know about this subject?

2. Read the Opening Paragraph. If the first paragraph is long, read the first sentence or two instead. The first paragraph is the writer's opportunity to greet the reader. He may have something to tell you about what is to come. Some writers announce what they hope to tell you in the selection. Some writers tell why they are writing. Some writers just try to get the reader's attention—they may ask a provocative question.

3. Read the Closing Paragraph. If the last paragraph is long, read just the final line or two. The closing paragraph is the writer's last chance to talk to his reader. He may have something important to say at the end. Some writers repeat the main idea once more. Some writers draw a conclusion: this is what they have been leading up to. Some writers summarize their thoughts; they tie all the facts together.

4. Glance Through. Scan the selection quickly to see what else you can pick up. Discover whatever you can to help you read the selection. Are there names, dates, numbers? If so, you may have to read more slowly. Are there colorful adjectives? The selection might be light and fairly easy to read. Is the selection informative, containing a lot of facts, or conversational, an informal discussion with the reader?

flying normal
towers
stage
migration. some
cruising pelicans,
time subtle
scientists
close

Steps to Faster Reading

STEP 2: READ FOR MEANING

When you read, do you just see words? Are you so occupied reading words that you sometimes fail to get the meaning? Good readers see beyond the words—they read for meaning. This makes them faster readers.

1. Build Concentration. You cannot read with understanding if you are not concentrating. Every reader's mind wanders occasionally; it is not a cause for alarm. When you discover that your thoughts have strayed, correct the situation right away. The longer you wait, the harder it becomes. Avoid distractions and distracting situations. Outside noises and activities will compete for your attention if you let them. Keep the preview information in mind as you read. This will help to focus your attention on the selection.

2. Read in Thought Groups. Individual words do not tell us much. They must be combined with other words in order to yield meaning. To obtain meaning from the printed page, therefore, the reader should see the words in meaningful combinations. If you see only a word at a time (called word-by-word reading), your comprehension suffers along with your speed. To improve both speed and comprehension, try to group the words into phrases which have a natural relationship to each other. For practice, you might want to read aloud, trying to speak the words in meaningful combinations.

3. Question the Author. To sustain the pace you have set for yourself, and to maintain a high level of comprehension, question the writer as you read. Continually ask yourself such questions as, "What does this mean? What is he saying now? How can I use this information?" Questions like these help you to concentrate fully on the selection.

Steps to Faster Reading

STEP 3: GRASP
PARAGRAPH SENSE

The paragraph is the basic unit of meaning. If you can discover quickly and understand the main point of each paragraph, you can comprehend the author's message. Good readers know how to find the main ideas of paragraphs quickly. This helps to make them faster readers.

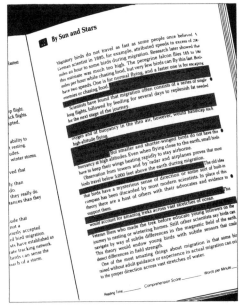

1. Find the Topic Sentence. The topic sentence, the sentence containing the main idea, is often the first sentence of a paragraph. It is followed by other sentences which support, develop, or explain the main idea. Sometimes a topic sentence comes at the end of a paragraph. When it does, the supporting details come first, building the base for the topic sentence. Some paragraphs do not have a topic sentence. Such paragraphs usually create a mood or feeling, rather than present information.

2. Understand Paragraph Structure. Every well-written paragraph has purpose. The purpose may be to inform, define, explain, persuade, compare or contrast, illustrate, and so on. The purpose should always relate to the main idea and expand on it. As you read each paragraph, see how the body of the paragraph is used to tell you more about the main idea or topic sentence. Read the supporting details intelligently, recognizing that what you are reading is all designed to develop the single main idea.

Steps to Faster Reading

STEP 4: ORGANIZE FACTS

When you read, do you tend to see a lot of facts without any apparent connection or relationship? Understanding how the facts all fit together to deliver the author's message is, after all, the reason for reading. Good readers organize facts as they read. This helps them to read rapidly and well.

1. Discover the Writer's Plan. Look for a clue or signal word early in the article which might reveal the author's structure. Every writer has a plan or outline which he follows. If the reader can discover his method of organization, he has the key to understanding the message. Sometimes the author gives you obvious signals. If he says, "There are three reasons . . ." the wise reader looks for a listing of the three items. Other less obvious signal words such as *moreover, otherwise, consequently* all tell the reader the direction the writer's message will take.

2. Relate as You Read. As you read the selection, keep the information learned during the preview in mind. See how the ideas you are reading all fit into place. Consciously strive to relate what you are reading to the title. See how the author is carrying through in his attempt to piece together a meaningful message. As you discover the relationship among the ideas, the message comes through quickly and clearly.

Timed
Reading
Selections

1 Water, Water Everywhere

Most people know that water is unevenly distributed over the earth's surface in oceans, rivers, and lakes. Few realize, however, how very uneven the distribution actually is. It is important to think of the total amount of water on the planet Earth, the areas where the water occurs, and the long-term importance of the findings.

The oceans of the world cover 140 million square miles of the Earth's surface. The average depth of the ocean basins is about 12,500 feet. If the basins were shallow, seas would spread far onto the continents. Dry land areas would consist mainly of a few major island groups with high moun- ●
tain ranges rising above the sea.

Considered as a continuous body of fluid, the atmosphere is another kind of ocean. Yet, in view of the total amount of rain and snow on land areas in the course of a year, one of the most amazing water facts is the very small amount of water in the atmosphere at any given time. The volume of the lower seven miles of the atmosphere—the realm of weather events—is roughly four times the volume of the world's oceans. But the atmosphere contains very little water. It is chiefly in the form of invisible ●
vapor, some of which is carried over land by air currents. If all vapor suddenly fell from the air onto the Earth's surface, it would form a layer only about one inch thick. A heavy rainstorm on a given area may use up only a small percentage of the water from the air mass that passes over. How, then, can some land areas receive more than 400 inches of rain per year? How can several inches of rain fall during a single storm in a few minutes or hours? The answer is that rain-yielding air masses are in ●
motion, and as the drying air mass moves on, new moist air takes its place.

The basic source of most water vapor is the ocean. Evaporation, vapor transport, and precipitation make up a major arc of the hydrologic cycle— the continuous movement of water from ocean to atmosphere to land and back to the sea. Rivers return water to the sea along one chord of the arc. In an underground arc of the cycle, flowing bodies of water discharge some water directly into rivers and some directly to the sea.

Recalling Facts

1. What is the average depth of the ocean basins?
   - ☐ a. 5,500 feet
   - ☐ b. 12,500 feet
   - ☐ c. 23,500 feet

2. How high into the atmosphere does weather occur?
   - ☐ a. three miles
   - ☐ b. five miles
   - ☐ c. seven miles

3. The atmosphere is described as a continuous body of
   - ☐ a. gases.
   - ☐ b. fluid.
   - ☐ c. particles.

4. The basic source of atmospheric water is
   - ☐ a. rivers.
   - ☐ b. lakes.
   - ☐ c. oceans.

5. How much annual rainfall do some areas receive?
   - ☐ a. 60 inches
   - ☐ b. 250 inches
   - ☐ c. 400 inches

Understanding the Passage

6. This article is concerned primarily with the
   - ☐ a. atmosphere.
   - ☐ b. ecology of oceans.
   - ☐ c. water cycle.

7. According to the author, most people realize that
   - ☐ a. water is distributed unevenly on the earth.
   - ☐ b. precipitation never falls in some parts of the world.
   - ☐ c. some lakes are deeper than oceans.

8. We may describe the author's style as
   - ☐ a. factual and informative.
   - ☐ b. light-hearted and humorous.
   - ☐ c. instructive and helpful.

9. The process of water returning to the atmosphere is called
   - ☐ a. condensation.
   - ☐ b. evaporation.
   - ☐ c. precipitation.

10. According to the author, a change in the ocean's depth would have an effect on
    - ☐ a. the size and shape of dry land areas.
    - ☐ b. our water and food supplies.
    - ☐ c. the delicate balance of the water cycle.

As soon as his plan had been approved by the men who had sent him to America, the young sculptor, Frederic Auguste Bartholdi, started working on the designs of the Statue of Liberty. By 1875, he had already made several small study models.

The most difficult problems were involved in the details of building. In solving them the sculptor had no guide but his own genius. The material must be light, easily worked, and of good appearance. It had to be strong enough to withstand the stress of a long ocean voyage. It had to withstand the effects of the salty air of New York Harbor. Copper was chosen as the ● material. The framework would be of iron and steel.

To get the form for the statue, Bartholdi made a study model measuring about nine feet in height. Another model four times larger was made, giving the figure a height of 36 feet. This model was correct in every detail. Then the statue was divided into sections. Each of these was also to be made four times its size. These pieces, when joined together, would form the huge statue in its finished shape.

Only a small part of such a gigantic statue could be worked on at a time. ● Section by section, the 36-foot model was enlarged to four times its size. For each section of the enlarged model it was necessary to take about 9,000 separate measurements. When a section was finished, the carpenters made wooden molds.

On these molds, thin copper sheets were pressed and hammered into shape. More than 300 separate sheets of copper, each hand-hammered over a single mold, went into the statue to form the figure.

The framework, too, is worthy of attention. It was designed and built by the great French engineer, Gustave Eiffel, who later constructed the famous ● Eiffel Tower in Paris. Four huge iron posts run from the base of the statue to the top, forming a pyramid that bears the weight of the whole structure. Out of this central tower is built a maze of smaller beams, each supporting many outer copper sheets. Each sheet is backed by an iron strap to give it stiffness. These iron straps are fastened to the supporting framework in such a way that each section is supported separately. Separately supported sections are part of the Eiffel Tower's elaborate structural design.

Recalling Facts

1. The Statue of Liberty was
   constructed of
   ☐ a. copper.
   ☐ b. brass.
   ☐ c. nickel.

2. Bartholdi's first study model
   of the Statue was
   ☐ a. three feet high.
   ☐ b. six feet high.
   ☐ c. nine feet high.

3. The framework of the Statue
   was made of
   ☐ a. iron and steel.
   ☐ b. iron and copper.
   ☐ c. copper and steel.

4. Molds for the Statue were
   made of
   ☐ a. lead.
   ☐ b. sandstone.
   ☐ c. wood.

5. The man who designed
   the framework of the Statue
   later built
   ☐ a. the Empire
        State Building.
   ☐ b. Big Ben.
   ☐ c. the Eiffel Tower.

Understanding the Passage

6. The Statue of Liberty is more than
   ☐ a. fifty years old.
   ☐ b. seventy-five years old.
   ☐ c. one hundred years old.

7. The selection suggests that, before
   building the Statue, Bartholdi
   ☐ a. had achieved
        world-wide fame.
   ☐ b. studied sculpture in Italy.
   ☐ c. visited New York Harbor.

8. The author feels that Bartholdi
   ☐ a. possessed creative genius.
   ☐ b. was too young for such an
        important assignment.
   ☐ c. learned a great deal
        from Eiffel.

9. According to the article, copper is
   ☐ a. rigid and thick.
   ☐ b. heavy yet easily worked.
   ☐ c. light but strong.

10. We can conclude that
    ☐ a. New York City paid
         for the Statue.
    ☐ b. the Statue of Liberty was the
         first of its type ever made.
    ☐ c. the Statue has been
         repaired many times since
         it was built.

3 Mammals That Never Drink

The mammals that live in Dinosaur National Monument in Colorado are almost never seen. Almost all of them come out at night, are small, and are very shy.

In spite of their retiring habits, they show themselves in a number of ways. Patches of bare earth under sagebrush and nearby sandy slopes are crisscrossed with tiny paths beaten into the dust by deer mice. Along the riverbank, gnawed tree stumps, a few fresh chips, and perhaps a webbed footprint tell us beaver have been active during the night. The paired hind footprints of the kangaroo rat are common on the hillside. Freshly fallen snow records the previous night's activities in great detail.

Were it not for the golden-mantled ground squirrels, our proof of mammals would be mostly indirect. But these little fellows are seen all day long as they play around the visitor center and in the picnic areas. They are handsome, too, with their alert black eyes, cinnamon neck and shoulders, and dark side patches with white stripes.

The water problem is an ever-present one for the mammals, as well as for the plants. At first this may seem strange with the Green River close by and several springs in the hills. But most of the smaller animals do not travel far from their homes. A deer mouse, for example, seldom travels more than 100 feet from his home burrow in his entire lifetime. The kangaroo rat and the desert wood rat also have limited ranges although theirs are a bit larger than those of deer mice. A large number of such animals must meet their water needs without springs or seeps. How do they do it?

The food they eat has some water in it. The green vegetation in springtime contains large amounts. Even air-dried foods such as seeds contain some. Through the thousands of years that these little creatures have lived in dry lands, natural processes have changed their bodies and life patterns to fit the conditions under which they must live. Surely one of the most useful and interesting of their abilities is that of using metabolic water. During the digestive process these animals are able to make water from the chemical portions of their food and the oxygen in their blood. Thus some animals are able to live a normal life-span without ever taking a drink, and many of them probably do.

Recalling Facts

1. Most mammals near Dinosaur National Monument are not seen because they are
   - ☐ a. nocturnal.
   - ☐ b. hibernating.
   - ☐ c. migratory.

2. The mammals that live near Dinosaur National Monument are
   - ☐ a. dangerous.
   - ☐ b. threatened.
   - ☐ c. small.

3. The animal providing the most direct evidence about mammals is the
   - ☐ a. mongoose.
   - ☐ b. kangaroo.
   - ☐ c. squirrel.

4. What is the greatest distance a deer mouse travels from its home?
   - ☐ a. 100 feet
   - ☐ b. 500 feet
   - ☐ c. 1,000 feet

5. The mammals of Dinosaur National Monument obtain their water from
   - ☐ a. springs.
   - ☐ b. meat.
   - ☐ c. vegetation.

Understanding the Passage

6. The mammals of Dinosaur National Monument demonstrate
   - ☐ a. survival of the fittest.
   - ☐ b. the importance of instinct.
   - ☐ c. the effects of evolution.

7. One type of mammal at Dinosaur National Monument is often seen by
   - ☐ a. scientists involved in ecology research.
   - ☐ b. naturalists looking for rare animals.
   - ☐ c. picnickers in the visitor area.

8. The author implies that a diet of seeds would
   - ☐ a. provide good nutrition.
   - ☐ b. reduce the need for spring water.
   - ☐ c. add bulk to the diet.

9. The author mentions the beaver as an example of
   - ☐ a. a mammal that is threatened by pollution.
   - ☐ b. a rodent that damages forest areas.
   - ☐ c. an animal that leaves evidence of its existence.

10. The reader may conclude that
    - ☐ a. Dinosaur National Monument is located in a desert.
    - ☐ b. all mammals are very shy.
    - ☐ c. ground squirrels never drink water.

4 Schizophrenia

At times, normal individuals may feel, think, or act very much in a way that is typical of schizophrenia. Often normal people are unable to think clearly. They can be made so nervous by speaking in front of groups, for example, that they will feel confused and forget what they had planned to say. This does not mean that they are schizophrenic.

Often schizophrenics show what is called "inappropriate affect." It is emotion that does not seem to be logical for the situation. For example, a schizophrenic may say that his mother has died and then laugh instead of cry.

Just as normal people might sometimes do crazy things, a schizophrenic very often thinks, feels, and acts in a normal way. Unless he is in a state of total confusion, a schizophrenic knows that most people eat three times a day, sleep at night, and take baths. He does have a sense of the common reality. Being out of touch with reality does not mean that a person is living totally in another world. Rather, there are certain aspects of his world that are not shared by anyone else and seem to have no real basis. Hearing a voice of warning talking each morning is not an experience shared by most people and is clearly a distortion of reality. But it is only a distortion of one part of the reality. Everything else may be in place. A schizophrenic, therefore, may appear quite normal much of the time.

There is a very common notion that schizophrenia is a split personality or a Dr. Jekyll-Mr. Hyde switch in character. This is not a true labeling of the disorder. A woman who is mean and cruel to her children and then kind and thoughtful to her neighbors is not necessarily schizophrenic. She is acting in a different way at different times, but she does have some control over her behavior.

A schizophrenic is not a drug addict or an alcoholic. He may use alcohol or drugs to help him deal with his problems, but schizophrenics do not use this means of escape any more than does the average person.

A schizophrenic is not simply a happy-go-lucky person comfortable with his madness. For the most part he feels plagued and tortured. He is very much aware of his difference and his agony. He is tormented and frightened by unusual voices and strange visions.

Recalling Facts

1. Not being able to think clearly is typical of
   - ☐ a. schizophrenics only.
   - ☐ b. normal people only.
   - ☐ c. both a and b.

2. The article says that a schizophrenic sometimes
   - ☐ a. becomes lost.
   - ☐ b. acts normally.
   - ☐ c. refuses help.

3. For the most part a schizophrenic feels
   - ☐ a. tortured.
   - ☐ b. carefree.
   - ☐ c. indifferent.

4. Schizophrenia is defined as a
   - ☐ a. Dr. Jekyll-Mr. Hyde switch in character.
   - ☐ b. distortion of reality.
   - ☐ c. continual attempt to escape.

5. To most people a schizophrenic appears quite
   - ☐ a. unruly.
   - ☐ b. nervous.
   - ☐ c. normal.

Understanding the Passage

6. Schizophrenics generally do not
   - ☐ a. understand the difference between night and day.
   - ☐ b. have a sense of humor.
   - ☐ c. live totally in another world.

7. A person who is kind to her children and mean to her neighbors is
   - ☐ a. probably in control of her behavior.
   - ☐ b. in the early stages of schizophrenia.
   - ☐ c. suffering from withdrawal symptoms.

8. When a schizophrenic acts strangely, he
   - ☐ a. is unaware of his behavior.
   - ☐ b. tries to ignore his actions.
   - ☐ c. is very much aware of what he is doing.

9. The article suggests that a schizophrenic sometimes
   - ☐ a. can lose his sense of sight.
   - ☐ b. fails to love those around him.
   - ☐ c. sees visions and hears voices.

10. The author's point is developed with
    - ☐ a. several case histories of schizophrenics.
    - ☐ b. professional viewpoints of noted doctors.
    - ☐ c. facts which dismiss common views of schizophrenia.

5   What is Black Lung?

On a frosty morning in the West Virginia mountains, a group of men wait at the mouth of a coal mine tunnel that cuts through the mountain. They are dressed as coal miners have dressed for ages. They are wearing protective helmets with cap lamps, coveralls, and are carrying lunch buckets in their hands. One miner, however, is adjusting a strange square on his belt. It is a small box from which comes a plastic hose that runs up to his chest, where it is clipped to his coveralls.

The device is a dust sampler. A tiny pump in the box sucks air continuously through the tube, and a filter traps the dust particles as small as 1/25,000th of an inch. Coal miners used to breathe a lot of dust like this, and it gave thousands of them a disease called black lung.

Until recently, only miners were concerned about black lung. This disease strikes as many as one-fifth of the coal miners in America. In 1969, however, the Federal Coal Mine Health and Safety Act set the first limits to coal mine dust.

Although achieving the low dust limits required by law seemed a difficult problem, the Bureau of Mines was able to prove that it could be done. Bureau experts realized that dust particles are so small that, in air, they behave just like a gas—just like the methane gas that coal sometimes gives off when it is cut. Methane is explosive, and there is a well-developed method for thinning it down to harmless levels and moving it out of the mine. Couldn't these methods help the dust problem, the Bureau wondered?

At the West Virginia mine, the "mantrip" arrives. It is an electrically-driven car only two feet high, made to operate in "low coal." The men climb in, lying beneath the protective steel top. After a ten-minute trip, they climb out where the coal is cut. A strong breeze ripples their clothes. Some of the men have objected to the stronger air currents, but they all know that this is the air that protects them from methane and black lung. Some of them begin to adjust the fans, causing even stronger air currents to capture the coal dust and sweep it away from the men. The miner wearing the dust sampler moves a cutting machine into place, and the day's work begins.

Recalling Facts

1. The state mentioned in the article is
   - ☐ a. Ohio.
   - ☐ b. Pennsylvania.
   - ☐ c. West Virginia.

2. How many coal miners develop black lung disease?
   - ☐ a. one-fifth
   - ☐ b. one-half
   - ☐ c. two-thirds

3. The first limits on coal mine dust were set in the late
   - ☐ a. 1940s.
   - ☐ b. 1950s.
   - ☐ c. 1960s.

4. Coal dust particles are so small they behave like
   - ☐ a. gas.
   - ☐ b. sawdust.
   - ☐ c. water vapor.

5. Coal sometimes gives off
   - ☐ a. helium.
   - ☐ b. methane.
   - ☐ c. nitrogen.

Understanding the Passage

6. A dust sampler looks like a
   - ☐ a. vacuum cleaner.
   - ☐ b. large trunk.
   - ☐ c. small box.

7. The "mantrip"
   - ☐ a. warns miners of danger.
   - ☐ b. carries miners into work areas.
   - ☐ c. seals off the mine before an explosion.

8. The miners know the air is being cleaned when they
   - ☐ a. feel a breeze.
   - ☐ b. smell chemicals.
   - ☐ c. hear a humming sound.

9. The author implies that
   - ☐ a. only one miner is in charge of the dust sampler.
   - ☐ b. soft coal is easier to mine than hard coal.
   - ☐ c. deaths from black lung disease are increasing each year.

10. The reader can infer that
    - ☐ a. the dust sampler was invented by an American.
    - ☐ b. doctors cannot cure black lung disease.
    - ☐ c. black lung disease is a serious problem in large cities.

6 Trouble in the Water

All ponds, pools, lakes, and swimming areas should have water safety devices, first-aid equipment, and emergency directions available. The "safety post" or "rescue station" is simple, inexpensive, but adequate for most nonpublic swimming areas. As usually recommended, it is made of an eight-foot post with a minimum of two feet in the ground. This may be steel or wood and round or square. Onto this post is fastened a bracket or large crossed nails to hold a fourteen-foot bamboo or other light pole used for reaching victims close to shore.

A life buoy or ring with fifty feet of light rope with a knot in the end is also hung on the post. This is used by stepping on one end of the rope and tossing the life buoy beyond the victim, then pulling it back within his reach.

The safety can on the top of the post contains a small, but adequate first-aid kit. To the outside of the can are cemented directions for first aid, mouth-to-mouth resuscitation, and Cardiopulmonary Respiration (CPR). These instructions are waterproofed with a clear lacquer to protect them from the weather. The instructions may also be obtained from the American Red Cross.

An inflated inner tube may be substituted for the life buoy. But because it cannot be thrown as far as a standard life buoy or ring, it is not as good. It may also become deflated.

If a person in trouble in the water is within reach, a rescuer must securely brace himself and extend a hand to him. A pole, a board, or an article of clothing can be extended. Otherwise, a life buoy can be thrown beyond the victim and can then be maneuvered back to him. If he is even farther out, a rowboat can be used. The victim must hold onto the stern of the boat, or board from the stern. If the boat has a motor, the propeller must be stopped before the boat reaches the victim.

As a last resort, the rescuer may swim to the victim, approach from behind, and pull him in with his hand under the victim's chin. This method should be used only with the proper lifesaving training. If the victim is unconscious, begin mouth-to-mouth resuscitation as soon as possible. The victim must also be kept warm. These instructions are by no means a substitute for professional training in first aid.

Recalling Facts

1. The safety post is recommended for
   - ☐ a. large public beaches.
   - ☐ b. resort hotels.
   - ☐ c. all swimming areas.

2. The height of the safety post is usually
   - ☐ a. four feet.
   - ☐ b. eight feet.
   - ☐ c. twelve feet.

3. Safety posts are sometimes made of
   - ☐ a. aluminum.
   - ☐ b. steel.
   - ☐ c. fiberglass.

4. On top of the safety post is a
   - ☐ a. siren.
   - ☐ b. telephone.
   - ☐ c. first-aid kit.

5. A person who is rescued by boat must hold on to the
   - ☐ a. bow.
   - ☐ b. port side.
   - ☐ c. stern.

Understanding the Passage

6. The light rescue pole on the safety post is usually
   - ☐ a. longer than the post.
   - ☐ b. shorter than the post.
   - ☐ c. about the same length as the post.

7. An inner tube is not a satisfactory rescue device because it
   - ☐ a. is too heavy.
   - ☐ b. often can become deflated.
   - ☐ c. becomes too soft in the hot sun.

8. According to the article, the American Red Cross
   - ☐ a. builds safety posts.
   - ☐ b. offers courses in water safety.
   - ☐ c. distributes first-aid information.

9. From the information provided, the reader can assume that
   - ☐ a. rescue stations are different from safety posts.
   - ☐ b. a safety post is easy to construct.
   - ☐ c. a safety post solves most rescue problems.

10. We can conclude that
    - ☐ a. the rescue method is determined by the victim's distance from shore.
    - ☐ b. most ocean beaches are now equipped with safety posts.
    - ☐ c. most people know how to administer mouth-to-mouth resuscitation.

The Peace Corps: A Success Story

Has the Peace Corps been able to bring about any real change? According to Professor McKim Marriott of the University of Chicago, it has. He says:

"When I first spent time in the Indian village I am about to describe, it was 1951. It was a very remote and conservative place, and I did not feel that change would ever take place there.

"The life-style was based on barley and field peas, gram, some oilseed crops, and poor varieties of wheat. Yields were quite low. Getting an adequate supply of water to the crops was done by leather buckets, bullocks, and men.

"The people were not getting much to eat, and they were always complaining about it. In hot weather, you would find every blade of grass dug up by the roots and fed to the animals. Few fodder crops would be growing. The farmers were busy harvesting their grain crops and did not have time to water fodder crops. Everything was scarce. Leaves were cut off trees and fed to the animals.

"First, in 1958, the 150 small plots of land that supported the 850 people of the village were combined into perhaps 75 larger plots.

"Then, in 1961, the first government tube well was dug, and it watered the larger plots of land with much less labor than was required by the older methods.

"In 1962, the third very important event occurred. A member of the Peace Corps came to the village and brought some improved seeds and some new kinds of fertilizer. His farming efforts were successful. The next season, eight or ten other local farmers tried the same methods and were also successful.

"By 1963, everybody was falling over themselves to get the new seeds and new fertilizers. They had been shown that it would work.

"Because of the continued success, the farmers were then willing to go into debt to drill tube wells, and they could pay off their debt in three years.

"Suddenly the village had some cash. New temples and homes were built. More money was put into individual agricultural developments. The village had an increased demand for skilled craftsmen and tradesmen. Education levels shot upward. In 1952 only five percent of the children were receiving an education. Today more than 50 percent attend school.

"Most important, the villagers have keen awareness that something special is happening in their village. They have pride and the desire to better themselves. There is now local creativity, and before, there was none."

Recalling Facts

1. The narrator, McKim Marriott, is a
   - ☐ a. writer.
   - ☐ b. social worker.
   - ☐ c. professor.

2. The greatest direct threat to the survival of the Indians was
   - ☐ a. poverty.
   - ☐ b. inadequate water.
   - ☐ c. indifference.

3. The Indian village is described as
   - ☐ a. isolated.
   - ☐ b. uncivilized.
   - ☐ c. unfriendly.

4. The 150 plots of land became
   - ☐ a. 10.
   - ☐ b. 75.
   - ☐ c. 300.

5. The population of the tribe was about
   - ☐ a. 40.
   - ☐ b. 200.
   - ☐ c. 800.

Understanding the Passage

6. This selection is primarily about
   - ☐ a. achievements of a community.
   - ☐ b. the origin and development of the Peace Corps.
   - ☐ c. applying for work in the Peace Corps.

7. The technology of the Indian village was
   - ☐ a. founded on a highly developed crafts trade.
   - ☐ b. limited to primitive agriculture.
   - ☐ c. concerned with the development of simple industry.

8. Great changes began to occur in the Indian village
   - ☐ a. after a new chief was appointed.
   - ☐ b. after the government dug a well.
   - ☐ c. when the Peace Corps gave large sums of money to the Indians.

9. The article suggests that McKim Marriott
   - ☐ a. studies the life-style of people.
   - ☐ b. helps people who are in need.
   - ☐ c. brings religious teachings to primitive tribes.

10. When the narrator first visited the Indian village, he felt
   - ☐ a. hopeful.
   - ☐ b. discouraged.
   - ☐ c. angry.

8   Building a Dinosaur

Ideas about what dinosaurs looked like have been developed over many years of work and study. They are a blend of the ideas of several people who have studied different bones of a single kind of dinosaur.

The first requirement for arriving at a good idea of the build of a reptile is a nearly entire skeleton. If too much of the animal's skeleton is missing, a serious error could be made. But if the left hind leg is missing and the right is located it is possible to establish what the other leg looks like. However, if both hind legs are missing, they must be restored according to a similar reptile whose hind legs are known.

After the nearly entire skeleton has been found, it must be collected with great care. This is a difficult job. And, for some of the large dinosaurs, three months' work may be needed. The specimen is first uncovered and the fossil bone is treated with a preservative such as gum arabic, shellac, or one of the plastics. A drawing of the specimen as it lies in the rock is made on cross-ruled paper. A trench two or three feet wide is then dug around the specimen. The depth of the trench is fixed by the width of the specimen and the nature of the rock.

If the specimen is too large to take out in one piece, as most dinosaurs are, it is divided into parts that are numbered as they are taken out. Each section is bandaged in strips of burlap dipped in plaster of Paris. After the plaster has set, the section is turned over and the bottom is sealed with burlap and plaster. The section is labeled with the correct number and the section and number are shown on the diagram.

When all of the sections have been bandaged and numbered, they are packed in strong wooden boxes and shipped to the laboratory.

The work in the laboratory is more involved than that in the field. Great care must be taken to be sure that the bones will be undamaged. In most cases the bones have been broken by natural causes as they lay in the rock before discovery. All the pieces of each bone must be thoroughly cleaned and glued together. This job takes a long time. A large dinosaur requires the work of three people for four or five years.

*Reading Time*_____   *Comprehension Score*_____   *Words per Minute*_____   29

Recalling Facts

1. In this article dinosaurs are referred to as
   - ☐ a. mammals.
   - ☐ b. reptiles.
   - ☐ c. creatures.

2. How long may it take to gather pieces of a large skeleton?
   - ☐ a. six weeks
   - ☐ b. three months
   - ☐ c. two years

3. A preservative used on fossil bones is
   - ☐ a. shellac.
   - ☐ b. turpentine.
   - ☐ c. formaldehyde.

4. A factor which determines the depth of the trench is the specimen's
   - ☐ a. weight.
   - ☐ b. height.
   - ☐ c. width.

5. Compared to work in the field, work in the laboratory is
   - ☐ a. somewhat easier.
   - ☐ b. more involved.
   - ☐ c. less exacting.

Understanding the Passage

6. Establishing the appearance of a complete dinosaur is
   - ☐ a. a difficult and time-consuming task.
   - ☐ b. a relatively simple job.
   - ☐ c. an impossible piece of work.

7. The author says that the greatest danger to the specimen occurs in
   - ☐ a. the field.
   - ☐ b. transit to the laboratory.
   - ☐ c. the laboratory.

8. Which one of the following events normally occurs first?
   - ☐ a. A trench is dug around the specimen.
   - ☐ b. An accurate diagram is made on cross-ruled paper.
   - ☐ c. The specimen is divided into sections.

9. The author implies that
   - ☐ a. scientists work independently on specimen reconstruction.
   - ☐ b. large dinosaurs require more time to reconstruct.
   - ☐ c. very few dinosaur specimens have been found.

10. We may conclude that reconstruction scientists are
    - ☐ a. paid very well for their work.
    - ☐ b. experts in photography.
    - ☐ c. very patient people.

The American Dream

On the village green in Lexington, Massachusetts, there is a statue of a minuteman facing the road to Boston. He has a gun in his hand as if he is waiting for the enemy. The man is smaller than one might expect—small for a man who did so much that day in April 1775. The paved highway he faces today does not look like the dirt road that ran past the green to Concord. Cars have replaced the British soldiers. The squeals of playing children have replaced the gunfire. Only monuments now mark the place where Captain John Parker said, "Stand your ground until fired upon." But if there is one place where a person can stand today and say, "Here is where it all began," this small patch of ground is it.

Early on the morning of April 19, 1775, Paul Revere raced past the green. He stopped just down the street at a house where John Hancock and John Adams were hiding from the British. Within minutes the town bell rang out the alarm. Parker and his 70-man militia formed two battle lines on the green. Four and a half hours later the "shot heard round the world" shattered the morning's stillness. "If they mean to have a war," Parker said, "let it begin here." The British did not want a war and did not wish to start one, but it happened. Two months passed before the American Revolution began in earnest, but the fighting in this village by a small group of armed Americans marked the beginning of a new era.

Spread across the mountains and valleys of the eastern United States are the battlefields and roads where the two great armies marched, the places they fortified, and the rivers they crossed. Each site played a role in the drama that shaped and molded a loosely knit group of colonies into a nation. Each helped form the dream that became the United States. Standing by a cannon at Yorktown, in Washington's headquarters at Newburgh, or in Independence Hall in Philadelphia helps us to feel a kinship to the people who were there.

There are still places connected with the American Revolution that are well kept. Americans have set aside historic sites and buildings and have built memorials where colonists fought for their freedom. These memorials provide information and real-life displays of America's past.

Recalling Facts

1. According to the article, the statue of a minuteman is located in
   ☐ a. Boston.
   ☐ b. Concord.
   ☐ c. Lexington.

2. In the minuteman's hand is a
   ☐ a. bell.
   ☐ b. lantern.
   ☐ c. gun.

3. Washington's headquarters was located in
   ☐ a. Yorktown.
   ☐ b. Newburgh.
   ☐ c. Boston.

4. How many men were in Captain John Parker's militia?
   ☐ a. 70
   ☐ b. 130
   ☐ c. 190

5. Paul Revere made his famous ride during the middle
   ☐ a. 1760s.
   ☐ b. 1770s.
   ☐ c. 1780s.

Understanding the Passage

6. This selection offers a
   ☐ a. portrayal of early colonists.
   ☐ b. discussion of Paul Revere's ride.
   ☐ c. view of early battlefields.

7. The statue of the minuteman suggests that
   ☐ a. Boston was the center of the Revolutionary War.
   ☐ b. people were not as tall as they are today.
   ☐ c. New Englanders were very unfriendly to foreigners.

8. The "shot heard round the world"
   ☐ a. was a minor local conflict.
   ☐ b. symbolized the beginning of the war.
   ☐ c. did not result from the firing of a gun.

9. The author suggests that the Revolutionary War
   ☐ a. unified the colonies.
   ☐ b. angered the King of England.
   ☐ c. inflated the cost of foreign goods.

10. According to this author, "the American Dream" was the
    ☐ a. establishment of new towns.
    ☐ b. creation of war memorials.
    ☐ c. separation from England.

10 Miniature Gardens

Indoor container gardening is an enjoyable activity. Growing plants in containers can be fun for youngsters as well as for the not-so-young. Containers that may be used are limited only by the imagination—aquariums, old bottles, canning jars, plastic toys, china pottery, or concrete tubs on a patio.

Vegetables can be grown in pails, tubs, or baskets. They may be grown on doorsteps, balconies, porches, or carports. A person needs only to choose a container, artificial soil, and seeds. Artificial soil is free from disease organisms and weed seeds and is very lightweight and portable.

Tomato or leaf lettuce plants grown in a proper container will not only be decorative and fun to grow but will also result in great salads. Onions, peppers, and even a cabbage plant may be grown in a container.

Terrariums are glass-enclosed gardens. Fish tanks, brandy snifters, old bottles of any size, even quart fruit jars, may be used. Terrariums can be fashioned as a base for a lamp. They can provide light to the plants as well as beauty to a room.

Many native and cultivated plants can be grown in a terrarium or bottle garden, especially those that need high humidity, such as African violets, ferns, coleus, and ivy. One can collect plants that are perfect for this use in the woods, if one is lucky enough to have woods to wander in.

A layer of gravel or pebbles should be put into the bottom of the container for drainage. One can dig moss from the woods to line the sides of the container below the soil level. The moss should be placed against the glass. Then a two-inch layer of synthetic soil can be put in.

The plants can be set in place. Dirt should not get on the inside glass walls or the plant leaves. The container can be covered with glass or plastic by using sticks, wires, or other tools. Once planted, the terrarium rarely needs water. It needs only indirect sunlight or artificial light.

Gardens in miniature are fascinating. They provide a chance to express one's artistic ideas. They may be miniature rock gardens, landscapes, portable rock gardens, miniature herb gardens, miniature roses, cactus gardens, and miniature bog gardens with insect-catching plants. Even well-chosen woodland flowers can be developed into a small wildflower garden for a city dweller.

Recalling Facts

1. Artificial soil is
   - ☐ a. heavy.
   - ☐ b. light.
   - ☐ c. dense.

2. African violets require
   - ☐ a. high temperatures.
   - ☐ b. direct sunlight.
   - ☐ c. high humidity.

3. The author suggests using terrariums as
   - ☐ a. lamp bases.
   - ☐ b. paperweights.
   - ☐ c. fish tanks.

4. The article mentions that indoor containers can be used to grow
   - ☐ a. carrots.
   - ☐ b. peppers.
   - ☐ c. potatoes.

5. According to the author, wildflowers
   - ☐ a. die in terrariums.
   - ☐ b. are too large for terrariums.
   - ☐ c. grow well in terrariums.

Understanding the Passage

6. A bog garden should contain plants that
   - ☐ a. eat insects.
   - ☐ b. require little water.
   - ☐ c. have very small leaves.

7. A layer of gravel is used in the bottom of the terrariums because
   - ☐ a. gravel contains minerals that plants need.
   - ☐ b. soil that is too rich will kill many plants.
   - ☐ c. most plants will not grow in soil that is too wet.

8. Using artificial soil will keep plants from
   - ☐ a. becoming diseased.
   - ☐ b. growing large flowers.
   - ☐ c. bending toward light.

9. The author implies that
   - ☐ a. any object that is watertight can be used for a terrarium.
   - ☐ b. caring for plants in terrariums requires at least one hour each day.
   - ☐ c. plants in terrariums do not need any oxygen to live.

10. An owner of a terrarium must be sure that the
    - ☐ a. plants are watered each day.
    - ☐ b. plants are never in a dark room.
    - ☐ c. container is covered.

11   Three Gallons of Goodwill

When life was less complex but sometimes more difficult, and transport was primarily pedestrian, salvation to a stranded traveler in the Swiss Alps was a stoic St. Bernard. Tales of this canine Angel of Mercy with lolling tongue, a mop of hair, and a keg of brandy to help lost souls are legendary.

Today, transport is essentially motorized, and angels of mercy are hard to find. Yet stranded travelers can feel just as hopeless as yesterday's victim of snow and bad luck.

What driver, at one time or another, has not been part of this drama? Your car has a blowout on the highway. You push it to the shoulder of the road out of the path of other vehicles. You look for a tire jack, then recall you loaned it to a neighbor. You raise the car's hood, then venture nearer the traffic to signal your distress. Cars flash by. Hours pass. If you're lucky, someone eventually stops. If not, you trek to the nearest service station, which could be miles away.

Where are the St. Bernards of yesteryear? Won't anyone help a stranded motorist?

A modern equivalent to the St. Bernard service of the past does exist in Ohio. The courtesy car service won't give you a keg of brandy, but it will give you three free gallons of gasoline to get you to a service station.

An oil company in Ohio started the emergency road service to help stranded motorists on the 250-mile stretch of Interstate 71 from Cleveland to Cincinnati. The program was established on a trial basis as a goodwill gesture to the public. At the same time, with the heavy mileage they built up, the courtesy cars proved good subjects for research by the company with different types of gasoline and motor fuels.

In mid-June, 1970, a fleet of eight all-white autos bearing the company trademark and the words "Courtesy Car" was assigned to patrol I-71. The drivers were instructed to stop and help whenever they saw disabled vehicles and motorists in distress.

Each courtesy car is equipped with emergency supplies of gasoline, oil, water, and compressed air, and carries tire jacks, fire extinguishers, and first-aid kits. The drivers change tires, put gas in empty tanks, tend overheated engines, pacify people under stress, and perform other basic repair work needed to make the stricken vehicles mobile.

Recalling Facts

1. The author calls the St. Bernard
   ☐ a. an Angel of Mercy.
   ☐ b. a Mighty Mongrel.
   ☐ c. a Legendary Wonder.

2. A modern equivalent to the St. Bernard service exists in
   ☐ a. Vermont.
   ☐ b. Colorado.
   ☐ c. Ohio.

3. The company that helps stranded motorists also
   ☐ a. runs a restaurant.
   ☐ b. sells gasoline.
   ☐ c. repairs cars.

4. The company had a fleet of eight cars in
   ☐ a. 1960.
   ☐ b. 1965.
   ☐ c. 1970.

5. Each courtesy car is equipped with
   ☐ a. food.
   ☐ b. brandy.
   ☐ c. water.

Understanding the Passage

6. The drivers of courtesy cars find stranded motorists
   ☐ a. after they are contacted by car radio.
   ☐ b. while they are traveling on the highway.
   ☐ c. during severe weather conditions.

7. When a disabled car is found, it is
   ☐ a. always towed back to the station.
   ☐ b. often abandoned.
   ☐ c. usually repaired on the spot.

8. Ohio's courtesy cars patrol
   ☐ a. dangerous secondary roads.
   ☐ b. high mountain roads.
   ☐ c. one main highway.

9. The author mentions the St. Bernard as an example of
   ☐ a. a dog that is native to mountain areas.
   ☐ b. an animal that adapts easily to the cold.
   ☐ c. a dog that rescues travelers.

10. We can conclude that
   ☐ a. people are often willing to help others.
   ☐ b. help often requires payment.
   ☐ c. winter travel is safer today in the Alps.

A Nation of Contrasts

Of the many peoples and events that have helped to shape our nation, the British have done the most. This work includes the Magna Carta, Shakespeare, the early colonists, and the English language itself. Great Britain is a nation that is small in size, yet it plays a very large role in the affairs of the world. It is a nation of both kings and common people.

Even the face of the land has great contrasts. There are green fields, rocky and lonely moors, forested mountains, and coasts carved by centuries of storm-tossed seas.

The people who live and work in this nation of contrasts are people of a hardy race. As early as the 16th century, British sailors reached the four corners of the globe. Other Britons walked the length and width of Africa to open that land to the world.

In this century Britons have shown this same spirit of adventure. Britons were the first men to reach the top of Mount Everest. Another Briton was knighted for his bold deed of sailing alone around the world in a tiny boat. These men stand for the millions of Britons who face the coming problems of the 21st century with faith.

More than 60 million Britons live and work on the 93,000 square miles of land that makes up the United Kingdom of Great Britain and Northern Ireland. It also includes the Isle of Man and the Channel Islands.

The capital of the nation is London, but there are actually two Londons. First, there is Greater London, an area of some 616 square miles which has more than seven million people. Then there is the city of London, built on the site of the old Roman village. This separate unit, run by an age-old company, houses the banking and business center of Great Britain.

The two Londons are crowded with people. But there are still out-of-the-way spots in the pleasant countryside where a visitor can spend an hour or a day alone.

From the earliest pages of its history to the present, the thread of British civilization can be traced in many ways. The story of this hardy race is told in bits of ancient pottery, in new and old monuments, in the books of the people, and in the deeds of a daring nation.

Recalling Facts

1. What continent did England
   open to the world?
   ☐ a. Greenland
   ☐ b. Antarctica
   ☐ c. Africa

2. The first people to reach the
   top of Mount Everest were
   ☐ a. German.
   ☐ b. English.
   ☐ c. French.

3. The population of the United
   Kingdom is more than
   ☐ a. 60 million.
   ☐ b. 75 million.
   ☐ c. 100 million.

4. The city of London was built
   on the site of a
   ☐ a. Celtic village.
   ☐ b. Saxon village.
   ☐ c. Roman village.

5. The author portrays Britons as
   ☐ a. intelligent people.
   ☐ b. adventurous people.
   ☐ c. friendly people.

Understanding the Passage

6. This article is primarily about
   ☐ a. the English countryside.
   ☐ b. industry in Great Britain.
   ☐ c. the people of Great Britain.

7. The territory of the United
   Kingdom includes
   ☐ a. several groups of islands.
   ☐ b. a small portion of land on
       mainland Europe.
   ☐ c. Greenland and Iceland.

8. The author implies that
   ☐ a. the city of London has very
       few modern buildings.
   ☐ b. Greater London is smaller
       than the city of London.
   ☐ c. most business activity
       is carried on in the city
       of London.

9. One Briton is famous for
   ☐ a. flying across the Pacific in a
       single-engine plane.
   ☐ b. walking across the African
       continent.
   ☐ c. sailing around the world in
       a small boat.

10. We can conclude that
    ☐ a. England is the smallest
        country in the British Isles.
    ☐ b. Great Britain offers many
        varied sights to the visitor.
    ☐ c. Northern Ireland was once a
        separate country.

The Bear Facts

A mother bear with cubs should be treated with more than the usual respect. Although she may appear not to care for her offspring, the chances are she is quite on the alert. It is not very wise to get between mother and babies or close to them. Even the larger and more powerful male bears appear to keep their distance from females with cubs. Unlike the bear in storybooks, the "daddy" bruin has no hand in caring for the young. In fact, he is one of the few enemies that the cubs have. Cannibalism among bears is simply one more way of getting food.

At birth the cubs are naked, blind, and very small. Each weighs less than a pound and measures six to nine inches in length. Usually there are two cubs and often, three. Four are uncommon and five quite rare. Some naturalists state that the mother is three years old when her firstborns appear. Others say she is four. Most seem to agree that the mother has cubs every second year. It is not unusual to find yearling cubs cared for by their mother up to their second summer. The mating season, in June and July, ends relationships between the mother and her cubs. The cubs, who are now a year and a half old, are left to take care of themselves.

During the less touristy autumn season, many park visitors ask the question, "Where are the bears?" Signs warning the people not to feed these animals are still posted along park roads, but few, if any, bruins stay in the vicinity of garbage cans and campgrounds. With fewer visitors, the "pickins" have been reduced also. But more important is the fact that nature's various wild harvests, particularly acorns and beechnuts, are now ripe. And bears are doing what bears have done for millions of years—feeding on mast, as these fruits are called.

For a number of years, and up to the time of World War II, "bear shows" were staged daily in some of the western National Parks. Thousands of visitors enjoyed them very much. Food, usually garbage from park restaurants and hotels, was hauled to a special area at a certain time of day. Bears were on hand in varying numbers. A ranger or naturalist was present to tell the people about the interesting animals.

Recalling Facts

1. The most dangerous bears appear to be the
   - ☐ a. males.
   - ☐ b. females.
   - ☐ c. cubs.

2. At birth, bears do not weigh more than
   - ☐ a. 1 pound.
   - ☐ b. 10 pounds.
   - ☐ c. 30 pounds.

3. How many cubs are usually born at the same time?
   - ☐ a. one
   - ☐ b. two
   - ☐ c. four

4. The mating season for bears occurs during
   - ☐ a. April.
   - ☐ b. May.
   - ☐ c. June.

5. Most experts seem to agree that a mother bear has cubs every
   - ☐ a. two years.
   - ☐ b. three years.
   - ☐ c. four years.

Understanding the Passage

6. The author mentions storybook "daddy" bears to show that they
   - ☐ a. have little resemblance to real bears.
   - ☐ b. are very much like real bears.
   - ☐ c. create fear in the minds of young children.

7. At one time people might find bears
   - ☐ a. refusing to take food from a tourist.
   - ☐ b. being hunted for sport.
   - ☐ c. performing for large audiences.

8. Naturalists seem to disagree on the
   - ☐ a. number of offspring a female bear may have.
   - ☐ b. role of the male bear in the family unit.
   - ☐ c. age of the female bear when she gives birth.

9. The favorite food of bears seems to be the
   - ☐ a. various kinds of nuts found in national forests.
   - ☐ b. garbage left behind by campers.
   - ☐ c. special food blend prepared by game wardens.

10. To make his point, the author uses
    - ☐ a. an emotional appeal.
    - ☐ b. biased opinions.
    - ☐ c. a factual presentation.

14 Society and the Alcoholic

Like all diseases, alcoholism responds to treatment best when it is found early. If alcohol is in any way changing your life, you need help now. Perhaps you are one of those few lucky people who can really stop drinking. If so, you are truly blessed. One of the first comments of alcoholics is that they can stop their drinking anytime they choose to. Very few can manage this feat on their own.

Alcoholics Anonymous is a group of recovering alcoholics who seek to help one another through the sharing of mutual problems. Group members can be reached easily by anyone wishing to discuss an alcohol-related problem. They make no moral speeches, and they do not provide welfare or jobs. AA has done more to help the alcoholic see his problem than any other group has done.

Society, after years of trying to sweep the alcoholic beneath the public rug of apathy and loathing, is at last facing up to the responsibility of dealing openly and fairly with the alcoholic. While laws against drunken driving must be as severe as possible to stem the death on our highways, the alcoholic should not be punished for the disease itself. Public drunkenness has been taken off the books of many states. Jail is not a place in which to cure the sick. The problem drinker needs medical attention and sound advice. Except when he is behind the wheel of a car, he harms himself first and foremost by a disease that has self-destruction as its logical goal.

In addition to helping yourself, if you need help, you can also help others. Don't push drinks on anyone. A person old enough to drink is a person old enough to decide if he wants to drink. Respect those wishes, always.

If you're hosting a party, don't try to see how fast you can intoxicate your guests. Also, never offer a drink "for the road." The time for going home is the very time when the guests should be most sober. Placing a red-eyed person behind the wheel of two tons of steel is a gross error in human judgment. You share in that person's fate.

Alcohol is here to be drunk. Drink it in moderation, but know what you are doing. When going out for the evening, plan ahead of time who will do the driving, not drinking.

Recalling Facts

1. The author feels that laws against drunken driving should be
   - □ a. lenient.
   - □ b. repealed.
   - □ c. strict.

2. According to the author, a drunken driver should be
   - □ a. fined.
   - □ b. ignored.
   - □ c. punished.

3. When the author asks the reader not to force drinks on anyone, his tone is
   - □ a. forceful.
   - □ b. humorous.
   - □ c. sarcastic.

4. The author states that a strong desire for alcohol is
   - □ a. a disease.
   - □ b. an escape.
   - □ c. an inherited trait.

5. Until recently, society has treated the alcoholic with
   - □ a. apathy.
   - □ b. concern.
   - □ c. openness.

Understanding the Passage

6. Most alcoholics say that they
   - □ a. can stop drinking anytime they choose.
   - □ b. do not like the taste of alcohol.
   - □ c. have no willpower.

7. Alcoholics Anonymous helps alcoholics by
   - □ a. encouraging discussion of drinking problems.
   - □ b. finding work for members.
   - □ c. providing welfare payments to members.

8. The main goal of Alcoholics Anonymous is to help drinkers
   - □ a. realize the extent of their problems.
   - □ b. live in harmony with others.
   - □ c. find the meaning of life.

9. The author implies that
   - □ a. most people do not like to drink alone.
   - □ b. many people drink for attention.
   - □ c. some people can stop drinking by themselves.

10. The reader can conclude that Alcoholics Anonymous
    - □ a. conducts meetings in most cities and towns.
    - □ b. is sponsored by the federal government.
    - □ c. is a United Fund agency.

15   Spaceship Earth

All of us are really on a spaceship—Earth. At this moment, Earth is moving around the sun at more than 18 miles per second. On board are over five billion people and a limited supply of air, water, and land. These supplies, just like the air in the astronauts' spaceship, must be constantly used, purified, and reused.

In proportion to Earth's size, the layer of air that surrounds our globe is no thicker than the skin on an apple. A shallow crust on the earth's surface has all the soil and water that will ever be available to Earth's people. This tiny envelope of air and this crust of earth and water are called the biosphere. This is the environment that our lives depend on.

The biosphere is a closed system because nothing new is ever added. Nature recycles all things. Water, for example, evaporates and floats in invisible droplets into the air to make clouds. This same water comes back to Earth as rain, snow, hail, or sleet. It nourishes the plants and trees. It trickles over rocks and into the rivers where oxygen in the air helps to remove impurities that it may have picked up. The rivers flow into the oceans, and the great water cycle begins again. The rain that falls is actually the same water that fell on dinosaurs 70 million years ago.

Today, Earth is in danger of losing some resources because of the careless way we have used our limited supplies. Thousands of years ago there were few people on Earth and they lived simple lives of hunting and fishing. As the number of people increased, and as the years passed, people learned to make greater use of the Earth's resources.

We must change our habits of polluting and destroying the Earth. Of course, we must use the air, water, and other resources, but we must learn to use these without destroying them.

We have to stop dumping our wastes into the air and water. Many things we now throw away are made from resources that can be reused, but can never be replaced. Even the smoke coming out of stacks often contains chemical substances that can be recaptured and used instead of being expelled into the air.

If we want to save the Spaceship Earth, we have to learn to cooperate with nature by using, and not abusing, the environment on which our lives depend.

Recalling Facts

1. The Earth moves around the sun at a speed of almost
   - ☐ a. 20 miles per second.
   - ☐ b. 50 miles per second.
   - ☐ c. 80 miles per second.

2. The population of the Earth is over
   - ☐ a. ten billion.
   - ☐ b. eight billion.
   - ☐ c. five billion.

3. The air around the Earth and the Earth's crust are called the
   - ☐ a. troposphere.
   - ☐ b. ionosphere.
   - ☐ c. biosphere.

4. Some impurities in water are removed by
   - ☐ a. gravity.
   - ☐ b. oxygen.
   - ☐ c. minerals.

5. How many years ago did dinosaurs roam the Earth?
   - ☐ a. 70 million
   - ☐ b. 100 million
   - ☐ c. 130 million

Understanding the Passage

6. The author compares the thickness of the atmosphere to the
   - ☐ a. bark of a tree.
   - ☐ b. paint on a car.
   - ☐ c. skin on an apple.

7. This article could be titled
   - ☐ a. Natural Recycling.
   - ☐ b. The Movements of the Earth.
   - ☐ c. Finding Minerals.

8. The rain that fell millions of years ago falls today because
   - ☐ a. moisture is often held in the atmosphere for many years.
   - ☐ b. the environment is a closed system.
   - ☐ c. moisture enters the earth's atmosphere from outer space.

9. The author feels that the earth is in trouble because
   - ☐ a. we have not used our natural resources wisely.
   - ☐ b. we have allowed a few countries to become too powerful.
   - ☐ c. nations are constantly at war.

10. We can conclude that the Earth
    - ☐ a. will someday collide with the sun.
    - ☐ b. may someday run out of water.
    - ☐ c. may someday be destroyed by pollution.

Don't Tread on Me

Carpeting is one of the most expensive items we have in our homes. It should be selected with care. We should not rush into the purchase of carpeting. We should shop at good dealers and compare their products, prices, and services.

Very low prices and unusual "package" deals should be avoided unless the buyer has checked them thoroughly.

This does not mean that good buys cannot be found. A buyer might get a very good price on a carpet that is not a good seller because of a color or pattern, but it may fit his needs perfectly.

Before one begins to shop, however, one should decide on the color scheme and mood for the room. Since furnishing styles can be combined, a person is not bound to an all-traditional or all-modern style.

Tweeds or shags are usually more informal while plush pile sculptured patterns and formal designs are best for formal rooms. Colors of medium intensity show soil the least and usually allow more freedom in the overall color scheme. Plush piles show footprints and traffic patterns more than dense piles of low to medium loops or twists do.

Density refers to the amount of pile per square inch of carpeting. To check density, one rolls the edge of the carpet back to see how close the rows and stitches of yarn are. If there are large spaces and the backing can be seen, the quality is low.

Fiber content is very important to carpet performance, care, and appearance. Wool, the traditional carpet fiber, is luxurious, springy, warm, and easy to maintain. It usually costs more per square yard than the synthetic fibers.

Acrylic fibers are most nearly like wool. An acrylic carpet is a good choice if one wants the look and feel of wool at a lower cost.

Polyesters have the weight and luxury of wool but are shinier and less springy. They are in the same price range as acrylics.

Nylon is the most durable fiber of the synthetics. It is tough and resists soil. Static electricity is a problem with some nylons, but newer types are available that are static free.

Room-size rugs are also very practical, since they can be turned to wear evenly and can be sent out for thorough cleaning. It is also possible to change color schemes more easily by moving rugs from one room to another.

Recalling Facts

1. Shag rugs are considered
   □ a. formal.
   □ b. informal.
   □ c. unusual.

2. According to the author,
   footprints show on
   □ a. sculptured rugs.
   □ b. plush piles.
   □ c. shag carpets.

3. The most expensive carpets
   are made of
   □ a. polyester.
   □ b. nylon.
   □ c. wool.

4. Static electricity is sometimes
   a problem with rugs made of
   □ a. wool.
   □ b. nylon.
   □ c. acrylic.

5. Density refers to the amount
   of pile per square
   □ a. inch.
   □ b. foot.
   □ c. yard.

Understanding the Passage

6. Some carpets do not sell well
   because they are
   □ a. made of inferior materials.
   □ b. designed with unusual
       patterns.
   □ c. not guaranteed by
       the factory.

7. A good carpet for a heavy traffic
   area would be made of
   □ a. acrylic.
   □ b. polyester.
   □ c. nylon.

8. A carpet of low quality
   □ a. shows variation in color.
   □ b. is often shiny.
   □ c. has large spaces between the
       rows of pile.

9. Rugs are sometimes turned
   around in a room so that they will
   □ a. wear evenly.
   □ b. not fade in the sun.
   □ c. not be affected by moisture.

10. Carpet colors of medium intensity
    □ a. are usually inexpensive.
    □ b. are difficult to find in
        large sizes.
    □ c. do not show soil as much as
        lighter colors.

17   Mintmarks

Mintmarks were put on coins as early as Roman times to indicate the Emperor's workshops where the coins were made. Roman officials could then tell exactly where the coins came from if a question arose about the coins' design or workmanship.

Each United States mint has its own mintmark letter except Philadelphia, which has none. The Denver Mint uses a D, and the San Francisco Mint has an S. By studying the coins in a certain region or city, U.S. Mint officials can get a good idea of the flow of coinage in our country.

Coin collectors find mintmarks on U.S. coins helpful. Because different mints make different amounts of a certain coin, the mintmarks tell how rare a coin is. Since 1968, mintmarks have been put on the head side of our coins.

During World War II, there was a serious shortage of copper and nickel in our country. Large amounts of these metals were used to build weapons to defend our nation. People were asked to save the tin cans that food came in and to turn them over to the government as scrap metal. People were asked also to save such things as coat hangers, bottle tops, and kitchen pots and pans. These household objects were then melted down in our defense factories to provide raw metal for building airplanes, cannons, and ships.

The Lincoln cent is made of copper, and the government decided to issue a Lincoln cent in 1943 without any copper in it. It was made of zinc-coated steel. Minting of the new pennies began in February, and by the end of the year more than a billion of them had been made. The copper saved was enough to make one and one-quarter million cannon shells. The wartime cents were produced in 1943 only.

Nickel, too, went to war. On December 8, 1942, a year after the bombing of Pearl Harbor, the wartime nickel was first put into use. The coins were struck at all three mints from 1942 through 1945. The mintmark was made larger and placed over the dome of Monticello. For the first and only time in our history, a large P was used as the mintmark for the Philadelphia Mint. The nickel metal was entirely removed from the coin and did not appear again until the war was over.

Recalling Facts

1. Mintmarks can be traced back to the
   - ☐ a. Greeks.
   - ☐ b. Romans.
   - ☐ c. Egyptians.

2. The only U.S. mint which does not have a letter today is
   - ☐ a. Denver.
   - ☐ b. San Francisco.
   - ☐ c. Philadelphia.

3. Mintmarks first appeared on the head side of our coins in
   - ☐ a. 1874.
   - ☐ b. 1939.
   - ☐ c. 1968.

4. During World War II, there was a shortage of copper and
   - ☐ a. tin.
   - ☐ b. silver.
   - ☐ c. nickel.

5. The 1943 Lincoln cent was made of
   - ☐ a. steel.
   - ☐ b. nickel.
   - ☐ c. copper.

Understanding the Passage

6. Monticello is mentioned as the
   - ☐ a. home of Thomas Jefferson.
   - ☐ b. location of the first U.S. mint.
   - ☐ c. image which appears on the nickel.

7. The author implies that mintmarks
   - ☐ a. reveal the distribution of coins in a country.
   - ☐ b. are often changed to increase the value of coins.
   - ☐ c. reveal much about the history of the United States.

8. The facts presented in the article suggest that
   - ☐ a. the need for the penny is disappearing.
   - ☐ b. America's largest mint is located in San Francisco.
   - ☐ c. coins require tremendous quantities of metals.

9. The world's first coins
   - ☐ a. were made exclusively of silver.
   - ☐ b. indicated where they were made.
   - ☐ c. carried the names of emperors.

10. We can conclude that the wartime changes in coins were
    - ☐ a. temporary.
    - ☐ b. expensive.
    - ☐ c. confusing.

18   The Speciality Is Barbecue

New Riegel is a quiet little Ohio village about 60 miles southeast of Toledo, Ohio. When someone mentions New Riegel, a quiet little German town is not the image that comes to the minds of those in the know. The name conjures up a certain magical, mouth-watering vision: mounds of juicy, hot spareribs and chicken coated with rich, spicy sauce. New Riegel means the New Riegel Café, the place that serves great barbecue; "the best in the Midwest," devotees say.

Spareribs and chickens roast slowly in the Café's steamy front window facing the main street. At the front door, the spicy fragrance of dinner tweaks your nose, and you can hardly wait.

Once seated, you can share a pitcher of beer or soda with your friends while the chef cooks your dinner.

There are no menus. The waitress can tell you in one breath what would be on the menu if there were one—barbecued ribs, chicken, or beef, served in a basket with french fries, buttered bread, and celery sticks—and a gaily colored washcloth on the side. There's shrimp and ham, too, but nearly everyone has barbecue.

The meal is simple, but very special. Some people drive great distances, passing a dozen barbecue restaurants on the way, to dine at the New Riegel Café. "I don't know what we're doing right," says owner Pete Boes with a kind of wonder that has not changed after over 25 years of great success.

One of the things he does right, of course, is the sauce, which is a secret. It contains over 25 ingredients, selected by Pete through trial and error. "I started the sauce by taste and did that for about a year. Then, I wrote down what I put in it, and now we just use the recipe." The "we" he refers to are his wife; Jerry Mathias, his "right-hand man"; and his four sons, who work after school or whenever they're home from college.

The patrons on any given evening represent a casual cross section of Midwestern life—well-fed farm families, joke-swapping salesmen, laughing little toddlers and tykes, young couples and old, and perhaps even a celebrity or two, unnoticed amid the bustle. The casual atmosphere promotes gusto and relaxed enjoyment. This is a place for big appetites, easy manners, and knee-slapping laughter.

*Reading Time*_____ *Comprehension Score*_____ *Words per Minute*_____   **49**

Recalling Facts

1. New Riegel is a quiet, little village located in
   ☐ a. Ohio.
   ☐ b. Arizona.
   ☐ c. Virginia.

2. The New Riegel Café is located on a
   ☐ a. secondary road.
   ☐ b. super highway.
   ☐ c. main street.

3. How many ingredients are there in Pete's secret barbecue sauce?
   ☐ a. over 15
   ☐ b. over 25
   ☐ c. just 23

4. How long has the New Riegel Café been in business?
   ☐ a. 5 years
   ☐ b. 12 years
   ☐ c. 25 years

5. Pete Boes's "right-hand man" is
   ☐ a. his son.
   ☐ b. his nephew.
   ☐ c. Jerry Mathias.

Understanding the Passage

6. The atmosphere of the New Riegel Café is
   ☐ a. elegant and formal.
   ☐ b. tense and businesslike.
   ☐ c. casual and friendly.

7. The famous barbecue sauce of the New Riegel was
   ☐ a. handed down through the family.
   ☐ b. discovered by accident.
   ☐ c. created experimentally.

8. The clientele of the New Riegel is a
   ☐ a. blend of farm families and salesmen.
   ☐ b. combination of college students and young couples.
   ☐ c. mixture of different types of people.

9. At the New Riegel one could order
   ☐ a. several cooked vegetables.
   ☐ b. a large steak.
   ☐ c. a basket of shrimp.

10. In this selection, the author makes the point that
   ☐ a. New Riegel is a famous industrial town.
   ☐ b. the New Riegel Café has made New Riegel famous.
   ☐ c. no other restaurants near New Riegel offer barbecue.

Laws have been written to govern the use of the flag and to insure a proper respect for the Stars and Stripes. Custom has decreed certain other observances in regard to its use. All the armed services have precise regulations regarding the display of the national flag, which may vary somewhat from the general rules.

The national flag should be raised and lowered by hand. Do not raise the flag while it is furled. Unfurl, then hoist quickly to the top of the staff. Lower it slowly and with dignity. Place no objects on or over the flag. A speaker's table is sometimes covered with the flag. This practice should be avoided. Bunting of blue, white, and red, arranged with the blue above, the white in the middle, and the red below, should be used for such purposes of decoration as covering a speaker's desk or draping of any nature.

The flag should never be displayed with the union down except as a signal of dire distress.

Do not use the flag as a portion of a costume or athletic uniform. Do not embroider it upon cushions or handkerchiefs, nor print it on paper napkins or boxes.

A federal law provides that a trademark cannot be registered if it comprises the flag, coat-of-arms, or other insignia of the United States, or any simulation thereof.

When the flag is used in unveiling a statue or monument, it should not serve as a covering of the object to be unveiled. If it is displayed on such occasions, do not allow the flag to fall to the ground, but let it be carried aloft to form a feature of the ceremony.

Take every precaution to prevent the flag from becoming soiled. It should not be allowed to touch the ground or floor, nor to brush against objects.

When carried, the flag should always be aloft and free—never flat or horizontal.

No other flag may be flown above the Stars and Stripes, except the United Nations flag at U.N. Headquarters, and the church pennant. This latter, a dark blue cross on a white background, is flown during church services conducted by naval chaplains at sea.

Many private citizens own and fly the American flag. In the United States, citizens may display their flag every day except when weather conditions are too severe. Customarily, the flag is displayed from sunrise to sunset.

Recalling Facts

1. The flag may be displayed
   with the union down as a
   - ☐ a. warning.
   - ☐ b. sign of mourning.
   - ☐ c. distress signal.

2. The author states that the flag
   should never be
   - ☐ a. washed.
   - ☐ b. touched.
   - ☐ c. soiled.

3. When the flag is carried, it
   should be held
   - ☐ a. flat.
   - ☐ b. horizontal.
   - ☐ c. aloft.

4. One flag that may be flown
   above the Stars and Stripes is
   - ☐ a. the U.N. flag.
   - ☐ b. a state flag.
   - ☐ c. the local church flag.

5. The flag cannot be
   displayed on a
   - ☐ a. costume.
   - ☐ b. casket.
   - ☐ c. mast.

Understanding the Passage

6. The author implies that the flag
   cannot be raised
   - ☐ a. in cloudy weather.
   - ☐ b. by mechanical means.
   - ☐ c. during a song.

7. The information in the article
   suggests that
   - ☐ a. there are varying sets of
     rules governing the display
     of the flag.
   - ☐ b. no foreign country may
     display the American flag.
   - ☐ c. the flag must never be left
     out at night.

8. When the flag is used in the unveiling of a monument, it may be
   - ☐ a. used as a covering on the
     monument.
   - ☐ b. raised while it is furled.
   - ☐ c. displayed above the
     monument.

9. Custom dictates that the
   American flag be
   - ☐ a. lowered faster than
     it is raised.
   - ☐ b. raised faster than
     it is lowered.
   - ☐ c. raised and lowered at
     the same rate.

10. Federal law does not allow any
    - ☐ a. company to use the flag in
      its trademark.
    - ☐ b. flags to be made by hand.
    - ☐ c. citizen to display the flag
      after sunset.

A backyard or some other space in full sunlight is the best spot for a home vegetable garden. However, poor drainage, shallow soil, and shade from buildings or trees may mean the garden must be located in an area farther from the house.

In planning a garden, one should think of what and how much to plant. It is better to have a small garden well kept than a large one full of weeds.

Many vegetables have colorful flowers. Some vegetables can be grown in a flower bed. Others can be grown entirely in containers.

The amount of sunlight a garden gets also is very important. Leafy vegetables, for example, can be grown in some shade, but vegetables that produce fruit must be grown in direct sunlight.

The garden should be surrounded by a fence to keep out dogs, rabbits, and other animals. The damage done by stray animals during a season or two can equal the cost of a fence. A fence also can serve as a trellis for beans, peas, tomatoes, and other crops that need support.

In most sections of the country, rodents damage garden crops. In the East, moles and mice cause much injury. Moles dig under the plants. They cause the soil to dry out around the roots. Mice either work alone or follow the holes made by moles. They destroy newly planted seeds and young plants. In the West, ground squirrels and prairie dogs damage vegetable gardens. Most of these pests can be stopped with traps.

Rich, deep, well-drained soil is necessary for a good garden. The soil should be well drained, well supplied with organic matter, and free of stones. The kind of subsoil is very important. Hard shale, rock ledges, gravel beds, or very deep sand under the surface soil will make the soil very poor. On the other hand, soil that has good qualities can be made rich. Using organic matter, lime, fertilizer, and other materials can improve it.

Good drainage of the soil is necessary. Soil drainage may often be improved by digging ditches and by plowing deep into the subsoil. The garden should be free of low places where water might stand after a heavy rain. Water from surrounding land should not drain into the garden. There should be no danger of flooding by overflow from nearby streams. Careful planning is important when developing a garden.

Recalling Facts

1. A garden should be located in
   - ☐ a. partial shade.
   - ☐ b. full shade.
   - ☐ c. full sunlight.

2. Vertical support must be provided for growing
   - ☐ a. peppers.
   - ☐ b. peas.
   - ☐ c. cucumbers.

3. Ground squirrels are often controlled with
   - ☐ a. poison.
   - ☐ b. traps.
   - ☐ c. fences.

4. What animal causes the roots of plants to dry out?
   - ☐ a. the mole
   - ☐ b. the chipmunk
   - ☐ c. the rabbit

5. According to the author, stones and rocks
   - ☐ a. retain moisture.
   - ☐ b. have no effect on a garden.
   - ☐ c. hinder plant growth.

Understanding the Passage

6. The author implies that
   - ☐ a. some vegetables have colorful blossoms.
   - ☐ b. most vegetables need a sandy soil.
   - ☐ c. a garden should not be planted near a building.

7. Green, leafy vegetables can be planted
   - ☐ a. along the bank of a stream.
   - ☐ b. in fertilized sandy soil.
   - ☐ c. in partial shade.

8. The author stresses the importance of
   - ☐ a. using organic fertilizer rather than commercial products.
   - ☐ b. digging the soil deep enough for good drainage.
   - ☐ c. covering the garden with straw during winter months.

9. Poor quality garden soil can be
   - ☐ a. used for flowers but not for vegetables.
   - ☐ b. improved with the use of lime.
   - ☐ c. mixed with gravel to improve texture.

10. We can conclude that
    - ☐ a. gardens that have good soil produce well.
    - ☐ b. most people think gardens require little work.
    - ☐ c. the most fertile gardens are found in the South.

21 Meetings With the Nobles

In 1066 William of Normandy invaded Britain. His armies beat those of King Harold in the Battle of Hastings. The Normans claimed the land as their own.

Knowing that he needed the full support of the Britons, the Norman king made few changes in their way of life. However, he made all the nobles swear their loyalty to the throne rather than to the local lords. In this manner King William made his throne safe.

William's heirs were followed on the throne by rulers from the House of Plantagenet. Many of the Plantagenet kings were wise rulers. It was the harsh rule and the high taxes of the third ruler in the line, King John, that led to a revolt by his nobles. These men forced the King to sign the *Magna Carta* at Runnymede in 1215. By signing, he said that the nobles had certain rights that a king could not take away. The first charter stated these rights for only nobles and certain freemen who held land. Through the centuries, however, they became the rights of all the men and women of Britain.

To help run the country, the British rulers held meetings with the nobles. These meetings, later known as Parliament, were held on a regular basis. And soon the nobles expected to be asked before new taxes were announced. As trade grew, the towns became more important to the growth of the country. Soon, leaders of large towns and churchmen were invited to sit in the Parliament. By the 14th century, Parliament was split into two houses. The House of Lords was made up of nobles and churchmen. The House of Commons was made up of townspeople.

The rulers of Britain were related to many of the ruling families of Europe. Through these relations, trading markets were opened with the countries on the Continent. By the end of the 14th century trade with other nations had become an important part of Britain's economy.

There was civil strife in the country. But through it all Britons continued to seek new markets for their trade. Rulers of the House of Tudor gave money to explore new lands in the hopes of finding raw materials. In 1583 a British colony was founded in Newfoundland. In 1585 the first British settlers arrived at Roanoke Island off the coast of what is now North Carolina.

*Reading Time*_____ *Comprehension Score*_____ *Words per Minute*_____ 55

Recalling Facts

1. William of Normandy
   defeated
   □ a. King Harold.
   □ b. King Henry.
   □ c. King Richard.

2. The famous Battle of
   Hastings occurred in
   □ a. 925.
   □ b. 1066.
   □ c. 1233.

3. According to the author,
   King John was
   □ a. well liked.
   □ b. respected.
   □ c. disliked.

4. The famous document which
   the author mentions is the
   □ a. Declaration of
       Independence.
   □ b. Mayflower Compact.
   □ c. Magna Carta.

5. The House of Commons was
   comprised of
   □ a. townspeople.
   □ b. nobles.
   □ c. clergymen.

Understanding the Passage

6. Rulers of the House of Tudor
   were concerned with
   □ a. internal strife.
   □ b. foreign trade.
   □ c. military power.

7. William of Normandy made few
   changes in the Britons' way of life
   because he
   □ a. was afraid of internal
       rebellion.
   □ b. respected British tradition.
   □ c. needed the support of the
       Britons.

8. Parliament had its beginnings in
   the early meetings between
   □ a. royalty and commoners.
   □ b. clergymen and lords.
   □ c. kings and nobles.

9. The author presents facts
   in order of
   □ a. importance.
   □ b. time.
   □ c. interest.

10. One of the earliest colonies
    founded by England was
    located in
    □ a. the West Indies.
    □ b. Newfoundland.
    □ c. Greenland.

22   Snow Rangers

The two things—snow and mountains—that are needed for a ski area are the two things that cause avalanches—often called "White Death."

It was the threat of the avalanche and its record as a killer in the western mountains that created the snow ranger. The first snow ranger started on avalanche control work in the winter of 1937-38 at Alta, Utah, in the Wasatch National Forest.

This mountain valley was becoming well known to skiers. It was dangerous. In fact, more than 120 persons had lost their lives as a result of avalanches before it became a major ski area.

Thus, development of Alta and other major ski resorts in the West was dependent upon controlling the avalanche. The Forest Service set out to do it, and did, with its corps of snow rangers.

It takes many things to make snow rangers. Snow rangers must be in excellent physical condition. They must be good skiers and skilled mountain climbers. They should have at least a high school education, and the more college courses in geology, physics, and related fields they have, the better. They study snow, terrain, wind, and weather. They learn the conditions that spawn avalanches. They learn to forecast avalanches—and to bring them roaring on down the mountainside to reduce their Herculean punch. Snow rangers learn to do this by using artillery, by blasting with TNT, and by the ticklish art of skiing avalanches down.

Snow rangers, dressed in green parkas with bright yellow shoulder patches, mean safety for people on the ski slopes. They pull the trigger on a 75 mm. recoilless cannon, ski waist deep in powder testing snow stability, or talk with the ski area's operator as they go about their work to protect the public from the hazards of deep snow on steep mountain slopes.

The safety they represent is not limited to their knowledge and their control of the avalanche hazard. There are ski lifts and tows to be checked for safe operations. For the work to be done with the National Ski Patrol to provide safe ski slopes, special-use permit requirements for public service must be administered. There is cooperation with area operators, ski schools, state road crews, and safety education for the skiing public involved—all a part of the snow ranger's job.

Recalling Facts

1. Snow rangers were established in the late
   - ☐ a. 1930s.
   - ☐ b. 1940s.
   - ☐ c. 1950s.

2. The snow rangers are an extension of the
   - ☐ a. Forest Service.
   - ☐ b. Resource Bureau.
   - ☐ c. Tourist Board.

3. A snow ranger must be a
   - ☐ a. college graduate.
   - ☐ b. mountaineer.
   - ☐ c. biologist.

4. Snow rangers first began their work in which state?
   - ☐ a. Vermont
   - ☐ b. Colorado
   - ☐ c. Utah

5. About how many people died in the Wasatch National Forest before it became a major ski area?
   - ☐ a. 100
   - ☐ b. 125
   - ☐ c. 150

Understanding the Passage

6. A snow ranger uses a cannon to
   - ☐ a. warn skiers of an approaching avalanche.
   - ☐ b. signal for help in an emergency.
   - ☐ c. create an avalanche.

7. The primary function of the snow rangers is to
   - ☐ a. make sure ski area operators are following safety rules.
   - ☐ b. forecast weather that causes avalanches.
   - ☐ c. predict and control avalanches in mountainous areas.

8. This article strongly suggests that snow rangers
   - ☐ a. are poorly paid for their services.
   - ☐ b. must know a great deal about science.
   - ☐ c. are away from home for long periods of time.

9. Avalanches are commonly called "White Death" because they are
   - ☐ a. inescapable.
   - ☐ b. unpredictable.
   - ☐ c. common.

10. We may conclude that snow rangers
    - ☐ a. travel many miles in the course of their work.
    - ☐ b. work under the jurisdiction of the National Ski Patrol.
    - ☐ c. must write lengthy reports on all phases of their work.

23　Today's Serpents

Only two of the 23 snakes in Great Smoky Mountains National Park are poisonous. They are the timber rattlesnake and the copperhead. In the Smokies, rattlesnakes rarely are more than four feet long. A few reports of rattlers more than five feet in length have been made. Chipmunks, red squirrels, gray squirrels, cottontails, and mice have been found in the stomachs of many of these snakes.

Hikers may cover hundreds of miles of park trails and not see a single rattlesnake. Yet this type can hardly be thought of as scarce or rare. If you should come across a rattlesnake while hiking in the park, the chances are ●
it will try to get out of your way. If it should hold its ground by coiling and buzzing, you can quickly cause it to quiet down by the use of a fairly long stick. These heavy-bodied, slow-moving serpents do not look for trouble. Danger from snakebite is greatest if you leave the trail in a place where there are rocky outcrops. In that case, be on the alert and watch where you place your feet or your hands.

It is also important to remember that these two kinds of poisonous ●
snakes may be active both day and night during the warmest part of the summer. Hikers should use a flashlight or lanterns if walking after dark.

Copperheads, although they do not occur as high in the mountains as rattlesnakes, are often found in the same kinds of places. In fact, the two species are known to hibernate together. A smaller snake than the rattler, the copperhead may be spotted quite easily by the hourglass pattern all along the length of its body. Copperheads are more secretive than rattle-snakes. A favorite hiding place is in old sawdust piles.

The largest of the 21 nonpoisonous snakes in the park are the pilot black ●
snake, black racer, pine snake, common king snake, and corn snake. Of that number, the last three are among our most handsomely marked serpents. The rarest snakes in the park are the mole snake, the black king snake, and the queen snake. The list of Great Smoky Mountains National Park snakes includes the eastern hognose snake, eastern milk snake, rough green snake, common water snake, and common garter snake. The last two are probably the most common types in the area.

Recalling Facts

1. How many varieties of snakes in the park are poisonous?
   - ☐ a. two
   - ☐ b. four
   - ☐ c. six

2. Rattlesnakes in the Smokies live on
   - ☐ a. mice.
   - ☐ b. bird's eggs.
   - ☐ c. insects.

3. Rattlesnakes seem to be most common in
   - ☐ a. thick grasses.
   - ☐ b. wooded areas.
   - ☐ c. rocky places.

4. The author describes rattlesnakes as
   - ☐ a. aggressive.
   - ☐ b. slow moving.
   - ☐ c. nonpoisonous.

5. What is the normal maximum length of most rattlesnakes in the park?
   - ☐ a. four feet
   - ☐ b. six feet
   - ☐ c. eight feet

Understanding the Passage

6. The author implies that poisonous snakes are
   - ☐ a. afraid of the dark.
   - ☐ b. most active in warm weather.
   - ☐ c. always searching for food.

7. The reader can assume that copperheads and rattlesnakes are
   - ☐ a. not enemies.
   - ☐ b. bitter enemies.
   - ☐ c. not found together.

8. According to the information presented, copperheads
   - ☐ a. live very long lives.
   - ☐ b. can be found in swampy areas.
   - ☐ c. are easy to recognize.

9. The author points out that the danger of snakebite is lessened if
   - ☐ a. the hiker stays on main trails.
   - ☐ b. vehicles are used in camping areas.
   - ☐ c. campers wear colorful clothing.

10. Hikers may cover miles of park trails and not see a single rattlesnake because
    - ☐ a. rattlesnakes are scarce in the Smokies.
    - ☐ b. rattlesnakes do not look for trouble.
    - ☐ c. most people do not know what a rattlesnake looks like.

24   A Mental Disorder

Schizophrenia is a word used to describe a complex mental disorder. It describes a set of conditions that are not constant, but ever-changing. It describes a way of behaving that is not general among all sufferers, but highly personal.

In contrast to many illnesses, it is not found in one part of the body. Rather, it affects all aspects of a person's personality—the way he thinks, acts, and feels. No facts hold true for all schizophrenics. In fact, it is possible for two people to be called "schizophrenic" and to show very different symptoms.

Each person looks at the world from his own point of view. If four people go to see a trapeze show, they might talk about it later very differently. One person might talk about the risks involved in doing tricks in the air. Another might talk about the beauty and grace of the act. Another might talk about the ropes and pulleys. And yet another might talk about the beauty of the performers.

A person found to be schizophrenic might see any one of these four images just as a normal person sees them. Or he might see laughing hyenas, instead of people, swinging on the ropes. Just as each normal person views the world from his own position, the schizophrenic, too, has his own views of reality. However, his view of the world is very different from the usual reality shared by those who are well.

The world of a schizophrenic may be timeless, flat, without depth, without form. Faces may seem to change. The kind, loving face of a wife may suddenly seem harsh and cruel. The schizophrenic knows that his wife's face has not really changed. But somehow, it seems changed. He may blink his eyes to try to see again his wife's loving smile. These are images that can come to bother him.

Very often he knows that what he is seeing is not true, but he cannot change his view. A schizophrenic girl described an experience as follows:

"I went to my teacher and said to her, 'I am afraid. . . .' She smiled gently at me. But her smile, instead of calming me, only made me more nervous. For I saw her teeth, white and even in the gleam of the light. Soon that's all I could see, as if the whole room were nothing but teeth. Terrible fear gripped me."

Recalling Facts

1. Schizophrenia is a word used to describe
   - ☐ a. a nervous breakdown.
   - ☐ b. unpredictable behavior.
   - ☐ c. a complex medical disorder.

2. The conditions associated with schizophrenia are
   - ☐ a. constant.
   - ☐ b. uniform.
   - ☐ c. ever-changing.

3. The article says that the schizophrenic suffers from
   - ☐ a. nightmares.
   - ☐ b. illusions.
   - ☐ c. convulsions.

4. The world of the schizophrenic may appear
   - ☐ a. colorful.
   - ☐ b. happy.
   - ☐ c. flat.

5. For the schizophrenic, faces may be
   - ☐ a. expressionless.
   - ☐ b. changing.
   - ☐ c. funny.

Understanding the Passage

6. Schizophrenics in general
   - ☐ a. show the same type of behavior.
   - ☐ b. have their own views of reality.
   - ☐ c. do not enjoy circus performances.

7. The author speaks of a trapeze show to
   - ☐ a. portray the schizophrenic's view of the world.
   - ☐ b. show an example of perfect balance.
   - ☐ c. illustrate differing points of view.

8. The author says that the schizophrenic is
   - ☐ a. able to control his emotions.
   - ☐ b. very tolerant of social criticism.
   - ☐ c. aware of his distorted perceptions.

9. The author presents the experience of a schizophrenic girl to
   - ☐ a. show how kindness can be misunderstood.
   - ☐ b. prove that schizophrenics are aware of their illness.
   - ☐ c. illustrate the schizophrenic's disrespect for authority.

10. The author views the schizophrenic with
    - ☐ a. mild criticism.
    - ☐ b. total indifference.
    - ☐ c. genuine understanding.

Instrument of Freedom

Many critics have told us that the auto should stand accused of a number of sins. It has, they say, ruined family ties, helped to destroy our cities, shifted patterns of trade and living, changed the social structure of the nation, and affected the economy.

It has been found to be a major factor in air pollution. Its parking lots and highways gobble up the landscape and steal away the last of our unspoiled natural regions. And we often wish we could find a way to get from here to there without having to cope with the traffic.

But does any of this mean that we're finished with the auto? Not by a long shot. We're just entering into a new and more mature relationship with it.

The problems, after all, have come about because so many of us have wanted cars so much. The auto wasn't forced on us. On the contrary, it has always been a tool of social change. It is the average citizen who has used the auto to break out of his or her economic or social mold.

For the farmer, it meant the end of rural isolation. For the factory worker, it meant a chance to live in a much better location. For the city dweller, it meant a chance to pull up stakes and give the family some breathing space in the suburbs.

We have wanted the auto, and still do, for the special kind of personal freedom it gives us. Public transportation, say the auto critics, is much more efficient for moving large numbers of people to city jobs. But it can't give us some of the things the automobile does.

How about pleasure trips to places where trains and buses don't go? How about exploring back country roads or coastlines? How about the accident that leaves you needing to get to a hospital or a doctor for a quick repair job? Or how about the decision to just jump in the car and dash off somewhere?

And there it is—what the auto is really all about—freedom. For millions of Americans the auto has been the symbol of free choice. As society gets more complex, we'll have difficult decisions to make. But give up free choice? This is not likely. It's what created this nation in the first place, and it has always been in our blood.

Recalling Facts

1. For the farmer, the automobile
   meant the end of
   ☐ a. heavy work.
   ☐ b. poor pay.
   ☐ c. rural isolation.

2. According to this author's
   views, the auto has increased
   ☐ a. pollution.
   ☐ b. mobility.
   ☐ c. insecurity.

3. Compared to the automobile,
   public transportation is more
   ☐ a. efficient.
   ☐ b. costly.
   ☐ c. flexible.

4. According to this author, what
   has created this nation?
   ☐ a. adventure
   ☐ b. free choice
   ☐ c. inventiveness

5. To this author the automobile
   is a symbol of
   ☐ a. security.
   ☐ b. status.
   ☐ c. freedom.

Understanding the Passage

6. The author develops the
   main point through
   ☐ a. a strong defense of
      the automobile.
   ☐ b. a fact-filled rejection
      of the automobile.
   ☐ c. interviews with noted
      transportation experts.

7. The author mentions the
   decision "to just jump in the
   car and dash off" as
   ☐ a. an irresponsible act.
   ☐ b. a juvenile reaction.
   ☐ c. a spontaneous choice.

8. This author states that man's
   relationship to the automobile
   ☐ a. is changing for the better.
   ☐ b. has come to an end.
   ☐ c. is doomed in the near future.

9. According to the article,
   the automobile
   ☐ a. was imposed on society.
   ☐ b. is a dangerous vehicle.
   ☐ c. is a force for social change.

10. The author is
    ☐ a. critical of the auto industry.
    ☐ b. in favor of anti-pollution
       controls.
    ☐ c. concerned about opposition
       to the automobile.

Rats, mice, and some other animals can become serious problems. They like the same kinds of shelter, comforts, and foods that people enjoy. If nothing is done to stop them, they will be more than happy to move in with people at every chance.

Rats and mice are real pests. They cause much damage in nearly every place where food or clothing is made or kept. They also spread many types of diseases to humans and other animals.

It is impossible to add up the money lost by the people in the United States as a result of the activities of these pests. Food that is ruined by rodents amounts to much more than they really eat. Besides the loss of money, areas that have many rats and mice are signs of unclean conditions. Our greatest concern should be to correct the conditions where humans live with these creatures.

Removing food and water is usually the first step in controlling rodents. Then steps should be taken to kill the mice. The only exceptions are dumps, where some of the mice should be killed before the area is disturbed. This keeps them from hiding in the waste.

To keep an area free from rodents, stored materials should be placed on racks eighteen inches off the ground. Food materials should be stored in places where rats and mice cannot get them.

Although mice can get along without water, rats need it every day. Therefore, removing the water can be very important in keeping rats under control.

Conditions that draw these rodents must also be removed from all areas in order to stop the mice from returning. It is useless to kill rodents without cleaning up all the areas first. People must be taught to recognize factors that draw rats and mice. They must know how to prevent the rodents from coming back into their neighborhoods. They should follow the basic rules of handling, storing, and throwing away food supplies and garbage. Only then will efforts to get rid of rodents be successful.

Using poison is usually the simplest and most common method to get rid of rats and mice. Precautions must be taken in handling poisons to avoid spoiling food. Food for humans and animals should be kept away from all areas where poisons are used. Poisons should not be placed where young children can play with them.

Recalling Facts

1. In order to survive, mice do
   not need
   □ a. minerals.
   □ b. protein.
   □ c. water.

2. Using poison to kill mice is
   □ a. costly.
   □ b. difficult.
   □ c. popular.

3. The author states that rats can
   □ a. kill pets.
   □ b. climb walls.
   □ c. spread diseases.

4. Mice should be killed
   before they are scared out
   of hiding in
   □ a. cellars.
   □ b. dumps.
   □ c. garages.

5. The article warns the
   reader about
   □ a. handling poisons
       near food.
   □ b. keeping poisons
       in cabinets.
   □ c. using traps where
       children play.

Understanding the Passage

6. According to the article,
   □ a. rats are more dangerous
       than mice.
   □ b. mice are more common
       than rats.
   □ c. rats and mice are rodents.

7. Rats and mice cannot destroy
   food that is stored
   □ a. six inches above the ground.
   □ b. ten inches above the ground.
   □ c. eighteen inches above the
       ground.

8. One of the simplest ways to
   control rats is by
   □ a. keeping water from them.
   □ b. storing food in plastic bags.
   □ c. keeping the basement warm
       and dry.

9. Mice are considered pests
   because they
   □ a. are noisy.
   □ b. destroy wood.
   □ c. ruin food.

10. We can conclude that
    rats and mice
    □ a. are difficult to control.
    □ b. prefer to live in dirty areas.
    □ c. are afraid of light.

27 The Peace Corps Today

The Peace Corps is changing. It is growing up.

You can still go overseas to help someone. That will always be the real idea of the Peace Corps. But now you can work in an agricultural job that fits right into your speciality. No vague ideas about making the world a better place; you can make a contribution doing whatever your experience and training enable you to do best.

Here is how it works. A host country decides that it needs irrigation specialists. A call is sent out to the Peace Corps.

The Peace Corps director thinks of the exact qualifications that the needed volunteers must have. If he believes that there is a good chance of finding such people, he agrees to supply them.

Chances are good for finding irrigators, and the American West is the place to look. Regional agricultural recruiters are notified, and they begin the search. They visit colleges and also talk to irrigation farmers. If they meet qualified people, they tell them of the job and ask them if they would like to apply. If they say yes, the first step is done.

The application is not an ironclad contract to become a volunteer. It simply means that the applicant is very interested. The Peace Corps, in turn, will consider his or her background and interests. Of the people who apply, those most closely meeting the requirements will be sent more information. They will be invited to take part in a series of further meetings and interviews. In this way, they learn more about the jobs and what will be expected of them if they actually become volunteers. Also, the Peace Corps can find out more about the person's own experiences and aptitudes.

The need for people with an agricultural degree or a background in agriculture is high, so chances of getting into the Peace Corps are very good. Often good jobs in international agriculture are vacant because there are no qualified volunteers to fill specific openings at the time they are available.

In any developing nation, agriculture is the point where all change begins and where all hopes for the future must be built. But before any progress can begin, people must have enough to eat.

An agricultural Peace Corps volunteer cannot change the world, but he or she is in a good position to help some of its people, giving them hope for a better life.

Recalling Facts

1. This selection stresses the need for people with backgrounds in
   □ a. medicine.
   □ b. politics.
   □ c. agriculture.

2. People who work in the Peace Corps are called
   □ a. recruits.
   □ b. corpsmen.
   □ c. volunteers.

3. According to the information in the article, the Peace Corps is
   □ a. growing.
   □ b. changing.
   □ c. struggling.

4. The article indicates that the Peace Corps has begun an appeal for
   □ a. teenagers.
   □ b. specialists.
   □ c. retirees.

5. If an irrigation expert is needed, he or she will probably be found in the American
   □ a. West.
   □ b. East.
   □ c. South.

Understanding the Passage

6. The tone of this selection is
   □ a. persuasive and convincing.
   □ b. factual and informative.
   □ c. exaggerated and humorous.

7. According to the article, the basis for survival in developing nations is
   □ a. establishing free public education for everyone.
   □ b. receiving foreign aid from concerned countries.
   □ c. learning to grow crops in sufficient quantity.

8. This article demonstrates that
   □ a. organizations like the Peace Corps are financed by taxpayers.
   □ b. African nations depend heavily on United States aid.
   □ c. the United States helps countries in need.

9. Filling out an application for work in the Peace Corps
   □ a. assures the applicant that he or she will be considered.
   □ b. guarantees placement in a foreign country.
   □ c. entitles a person to an interview.

10. In discussing the Peace Corps today, the author arranges information in order of
    □ a. importance.
    □ b. interest.
    □ c. time.

28 Cosmetics

Many cosmetics sold today are labeled as hypoallergenic. This means that they can be used by a large number of people who may be allergic to the ingredients in other cosmetics.

However, just because a company says that a product is hypoallergenic does not make it so. The idea of hypoallergenic cosmetics is so unclear that it does not give any real protection for the user.

If you have allergies, the best way to make sure you are buying a cosmetic that you can use safely is to buy small amounts at first. Test the product. Use a little of it on your arm. If it causes a problem, then you know you shouldn't buy any more.

Cosmetics are generally safe if used according to the instructions on the label. But cosmetics, like any other product, can be harmful if they are not used correctly.

Before using any cosmetic, read the label carefully and follow directions exactly. This is very important when using antiperspirants, hair-removing products, hair dyes and colors, home permanents, and skin packs.

To see if you are allergic to a cosmetic, apply a small amount on the inside of your forearm. Leave it for 24 hours. If you notice any redness or blisters, don't use it again. In the case of hair preparations, do a patch test. Use it as directed on one small area of the hair and scalp to see whether there is a problem before using it for the entire area. Be very careful using eye cosmetics to avoid possible damage to the eyes.

If a cosmetic causes any burning, breaking out, stinging, or itching, stop using it. If the condition seems to be serious, see your doctor. Report any problems to the company that makes the product and to the FDA. You will be doing a public service.

Don't let children play with cosmetics. Keep cosmetics out of their reach.

Cosmetics are very important to our well-being. When we feel attractive, we feel accepted and secure. But cosmetics cannot change us permanently. They cannot make us suddenly look younger, make our bodies healthier, or prevent wrinkles.

When you're buying cosmetics, keep in mind that they are made to bring out your good features or cover up some flaws. But they cannot make you over, nor can they assure your living happily ever after.

*Reading Time*_____   *Comprehension Score*_____   *Words per Minute*_____   69

Recalling Facts

1. The concept of hypoallergenic
   cosmetics is
   □ a. precise.
   □ b. misleading.
   □ c. vague.

2. It is very important to follow
   label instructions for
   □ a. nail polishes.
   □ b. antiperspirants.
   □ c. hand creams.

3. To test a cosmetic for safety,
   one should leave it on the
   skin for
   □ a. 6 hours.
   □ b. 12 hours.
   □ c. 24 hours.

4. A patch test is a good
   way to test
   □ a. hair colors.
   □ b. lipsticks.
   □ c. powders.

5. Adverse effects from
   cosmetics can be
   reported to the
   □ a. Attorney General.
   □ b. FDA.
   □ c. Congress.

Understanding the Passage

6. The author points out that
   cosmetics
   □ a. can cause blindness.
   □ b. improve our self-image.
   □ c. are unnecessary for men.

7. The author warns that
   cosmetics cannot
   □ a. improve a person's health.
   □ b. make us feel attractive.
   □ c. enhance a person's good
   features.

8. In writing this passage,
   the author uses
   □ a. limited facts.
   □ b. interesting interviews.
   □ c. excellent comparisons.

9. The author is concerned
   mostly with
   □ a. specially formulated
   cosmetics.
   □ b. cosmetics in general.
   □ c. the use of imported
   cosmetics.

10. Cosmetics present a threat to a
    person's health because of their
    □ a. application.
    □ b. ingredients.
    □ c. overuse.

29 Due Process of Law

There are many legal rights to make sure that people will be treated fairly when they are suspected or accused of a crime. Sometimes these rights are called "due process of law." In using these rights, a person should have the help of a lawyer.

You are protected against unreasonable searches and seizures. Generally, the police may not search you or your home, or take things you own, without a "warrant." A warrant is a paper that states, very exactly, the place to be searched and the things to be taken. Sometimes, however, the police will not need a warrant to search you or your property. If an officer sees you committing a crime, or if he has good cause to believe you have committed a serious crime, he may arrest you and search you and the area right around you without a warrant.

If you invite a policeman without a warrant to come into your home and he finds proof of crime, the evidence may be used against you in court. If you do not want an officer to search you or your home and he does not have a warrant, tell him that you do not give him the right to search. However, if the officer will not listen, do not try to stop him. It is dangerous to resist and it may be illegal to do so. Any evidence which a policeman gets during an unlawful search and seizure cannot be used against you.

Police must act reasonably and fairly at all times. They should use physical force only when it is needed to arrest someone or enforce a law. Police may not use physical violence to "teach someone a lesson."

In all serious criminal cases you will get a lawyer free if you cannot afford one. You should ask for a lawyer as soon as you are arrested and when you are first brought before a judge.

No person can be forced to be a witness against himself. When in police custody, you do not have to answer questions that might help convict you of a crime. This means you may remain silent. You also may refuse to answer questions unless a lawyer is present. If you give information about a crime or confess to a crime because you were forced to do so, the information or statement cannot be used against you in court.

---

*Reading Time*_____ *Comprehension Score*_____ *Words per Minute*_____

Recalling Facts

1. A person can legally refuse to testify against
   - ☐ a. a relative.
   - ☐ b. a husband or wife.
   - ☐ c. himself.

2. For an officer to search you without a warrant he must have
   - ☐ a. a judge's approval.
   - ☐ b. your permission.
   - ☐ c. court transcripts.

3. If you are arrested, you should ask first to see
   - ☐ a. the evidence.
   - ☐ b. the warrant.
   - ☐ c. a lawyer.

4. You may remain silent when asked a question if you are
   - ☐ a. in police custody.
   - ☐ b. in court.
   - ☐ c. before a judge.

5. A lawyer is provided if you cannot afford one in
   - ☐ a. civil cases.
   - ☐ b. misdemeanor cases.
   - ☐ c. criminal cases.

Understanding the Passage

6. This selection could have been titled
   - ☐ a. A Day in Court.
   - ☐ b. Search Warrants.
   - ☐ c. Rights of Citizens.

7. The selection shows that the author is in favor of
   - ☐ a. court reform.
   - ☐ b. due process of law.
   - ☐ c. better pay for lawyers.

8. We can infer from this selection that
   - ☐ a. laws also protect people accused of crimes.
   - ☐ b. once caught, criminals usually cooperate with the police.
   - ☐ c. the police often search homes without court approval.

9. According to this article, a "warrant" is a
   - ☐ a. cruel deception.
   - ☐ b. legal document.
   - ☐ c. personal appeal.

10. This selection is meant to be
   - ☐ a. humorous.
   - ☐ b. sarcastic.
   - ☐ c. informative.

The tourist crush is over in Rome. The *Closed for Vacation* signs of late summer have been put away for another year.

The Romans themselves come back home in September after warm, restful months at the beaches. The city opens up. Sidewalk cafes by the hundreds are back in business, each with its own post-holiday specialties.

Most of the foreign crowds have gone. It's now a Rome for the Romans.

A stroll along the Via Margutta, near Piazza di Spagna where the Spanish Steps are located, finds the throng of tourists gone. Instead, traveling artists and writers visit the area. All over Rome art galleries are having openings for the fall season. Sounds of English, German, and French are heard.

Rome is in its fullest glory in the autumn. Its people are tanned, airy, and happier than usual. Top restaurants in Trastevere, the colorful old section across the Tiber, and elsewhere in the city are again in full swing, along with the discotheques and nightclubs.

At outdoor restaurants in the evenings, the rich forget they are rich, and the poor forget they are poor. Tables are heavy with food and wine. People talk, laugh, and sing with their neighbors. The traveler will find language no problem, especially after the first glass of wine together. The Romans will use any manner to express themselves.

It's an ideal time to visit the always-green Tivoli and Borghese gardens and the ruins of ancient Rome. For the most part, they're quiet after the summer season. This is the best time to get the feel of that centuries-old civilization. Visiting Rome in the quiet season also gives time for quick side trips to Naples, Capri, and Florence.

It's pleasant weather, too; just cool enough for a light coat. When November comes, the temperature starts to dip, and until the end of February an overcoat is needed. If by some chance it does snow at all, it melts almost immediately. Warm winds off the African desert can bring mild weather on many winter days. Many tourists plan holidays year-round due to the fine weather.

The real joy of Rome's winter is the Christmas season. The marvelous Sistene Chapel Choir and the Pontifical Superior School of Sacred Music can be seen and heard. Practically every basilica, church, or chapel welcomes worshipers with a chorus of majestic music and Gregorian chants.

Recalling Facts

1. The Spanish Steps are noted
   for their
   - ☐ a. pigeons.
   - ☐ b. artists.
   - ☐ c. restaurants.

2. Romans seem happiest during
   - ☐ a. spring.
   - ☐ b. summer.
   - ☐ c. autumn.

3. Famous gardens are
   located in
   - ☐ a. Naples.
   - ☐ b. Capri.
   - ☐ c. Tivoli.

4. Rome is often warmed in
   winter by winds from
   - ☐ a. eastern Spain.
   - ☐ b. the African desert.
   - ☐ c. the Swiss Alps.

5. During the winter months, a
   resident of Rome would not
   find many
   - ☐ a. open restaurants.
   - ☐ b. foreign tourists.
   - ☐ c. green gardens.

Understanding the Passage

6. The author states that snow
   in Rome is
   - ☐ a. unheard of.
   - ☐ b. very rare.
   - ☐ c. quite common.

7. This article is probably from a
   - ☐ a. travel brochure.
   - ☐ b. history book.
   - ☐ c. report about European
     customs.

8. The author implies that
   - ☐ a. Naples is located near Rome.
   - ☐ b. Florence is a small island.
   - ☐ c. Rome is located in
     northern Italy.

9. The author is enthusiastic
   about the
   - ☐ a. ancient ruins of Rome.
   - ☐ b. Christmas season in Rome.
   - ☐ c. art museums in Rome.

10. We can conclude that Rome is
    - ☐ a. a pleasant place to visit in
      the winter.
    - ☐ b. very expensive to visit
      in the fall.
    - ☐ c. crowded during the
      spring months.

Few desert travelers today are like the hardy souls of years gone by. People of all ages and from all walks of life go to the desert for fun. The desert is beautiful and interesting. But to the unprepared traveler who finds himself stranded without water, it can be a nightmare and a killer. Lost, thirsty, with nothing but cactus for company, he may think it impossible to find water.

Actually the Ancient Mariner's words, "Water, water everywhere, nor any drop to drink," are usually true, even in the desert. But there is water in desert soils and always in living plants. The trick is to get it. With a piece of plastic film, a person can build a simple solar still and get a drink of water from the desert soil and plants.

All the necessary parts for the "survival still" can be carried in a pocket. These parts are a piece of clear plastic film about six feet square; a second, but smaller piece of film, aluminum foil, or other waterproof material to use as a container; and a plastic drinking straw.

To make the still, the desert traveler must dig a bowl-shaped pit about three feet across and about two feet deep in the soil. The small piece of plastic film or aluminum foil is used to make a container in the center of the hole. The straw must be put into the container and stretched out of the pit.

Pieces of cactus or other plant material should be arranged around the side of the pit, and the clear plastic film is spread over the top. Some soil might be needed around the edge of the plastic to hold it down, and then a rock should be placed in the center of the plastic. The rock must be pushed downward until it is about one foot below the soil surface. The rock should be directly over the container. The still is now complete.

If the sun is shining, drops of water will form on the bottom side of the plastic film in about thirty minutes. In about an hour the drops will run toward the point of the cone and fall into the container. In four hours about half a pint of water will be in the container. During the day, about two pints of water will collect; during the night, about one pint is a typical yield.

Recalling Facts

1. A desert "survival still" consists of a piece of plastic
   - ☐ a. three feet square.
   - ☐ b. six feet square.
   - ☐ c. twelve feet square.

2. How much time is needed to collect a half pint of water?
   - ☐ a. one hour
   - ☐ b. two hours
   - ☐ c. four hours

3. The author mentions a famous quote by
   - ☐ a. the Ancient Mariner.
   - ☐ b. Shakespeare.
   - ☐ c. the Desert Fox.

4. How deep should the bowl-shaped pit be dug?
   - ☐ a. one foot
   - ☐ b. two feet
   - ☐ c. four feet

5. A small piece of aluminum is used to
   - ☐ a. reflect the sun.
   - ☐ b. scoop the sand.
   - ☐ c. collect the water.

Understanding the Passage

6. The author suggests using a rock in the "survival still" to
   - ☐ a. hold the plastic firmly around the edge of the pit.
   - ☐ b. keep the straw from falling into the pit.
   - ☐ c. allow the water to drip from one central point.

7. The "survival still" described in the article is
   - ☐ a. expensive but necessary.
   - ☐ b. simple and inexpensive.
   - ☐ c. elaborate but useful.

8. One tool that might make the "survival still" easier to build is
   - ☐ a. a hammer.
   - ☐ b. an axe.
   - ☐ c. a shovel.

9. From the information in the article, the reader can assume that
   - ☐ a. plants give off water vapor.
   - ☐ b. desert soils do not contain water.
   - ☐ c. cactus plants are safe to eat.

10. The author states that the "survival still"
    - ☐ a. cannot be used on cloudy days.
    - ☐ b. collects water after sunset.
    - ☐ c. works best before noon.

32 The Christmas Tree

One of the first questions a Christmas tree buyer asks is, "Where should I get my tree?" If you live in a large city or in the suburbs, you may decide to go to a local Christmas tree lot. These are set up for the sale of trees during the November-December period. Or you may want to go directly to a Christmas tree farm where you can choose and cut your own tree. More and more of these places are available today, and it makes a fine outing for the family. If you live in a smaller town, you may not have many ● choices.

Probably the first thing to look for is a tree with good, fresh, live, green needles that are soft to the touch, pliable, and yet not droopy. The second thing to look for is a tree that has good shape, a straight stem, and good even taper. If the tree is used in the living room in front of a window, it has to have two good faces. Select a tree with a straight stem so it can be put in a Christmas tree stand and will stay erect. The twigs should be stiff enough so they can be easily decorated, yet still not sag with the weight ● of the decorations. The entire family can get involved in choosing the tree that will satisfy everyone.

Once you have a tree, shake the tree well to get rid of dead needles and pieces of grass and weeds before taking it into the house. For best results, make a fresh cut at the base of your tree—an angling cut at about a 30 to 40 degree angle. Then place the tree in a container of water. This is a good safeguard against the needles drying out and becoming a fire danger. ●

Keep in mind that these trees are at a severe disadvantage, since they are put in heated rooms where low humidity exists, and yet they are expected to remain fresh, beautiful, and green. Without water, they will become dry, brittle, brown, and dangerous. A good-sized and vigorous tree will use a quart or more of water daily. The water supply should be replaced each day in the stand at the base of the tree.

Some people have suggested putting chemicals into the water to reduce the fire danger, but plain tap water is satisfactory.

Recalling Facts

1. The article states that shaking a tree gets rid of
   - ☐ a. live bugs.
   - ☐ b. excess water.
   - ☐ c. dead needles.

2. The angle of the cut at the base of a fresh tree should be
   - ☐ a. 10 degrees.
   - ☐ b. 30 degrees.
   - ☐ c. 45 degrees.

3. How much water does a good-sized tree need each day?
   - ☐ a. about a cup
   - ☐ b. about a pint
   - ☐ c. about a quart

4. To keep a Christmas tree fresh, the author advises the use of
   - ☐ a. tap water.
   - ☐ b. distilled water.
   - ☐ c. rainwater.

5. Heated rooms cause a tree to
   - ☐ a. develop disease.
   - ☐ b. dry out.
   - ☐ c. stay fresh.

Understanding the Passage

6. This article
   - ☐ a. presents a brief history of Christmas trees.
   - ☐ b. discusses how to select and care for a Christmas tree.
   - ☐ c. shows how to locate good Christmas trees in wooded areas.

7. The author implies that Christmas tree dealers
   - ☐ a. make very little profit on each tree.
   - ☐ b. probably work at other jobs ten months a year.
   - ☐ c. try to sell trees of poor quality.

8. A fresh tree
   - ☐ a. has a good shape.
   - ☐ b. is soft to touch.
   - ☐ c. has stiff needles.

9. The author feels that children
   - ☐ a. should help pick out a tree.
   - ☐ b. should not be allowed on tree lots.
   - ☐ c. know very little about the dangers of Christmas trees.

10. The author feels that using a chemical to increase a tree's fire resistance is
    - ☐ a. not really necessary.
    - ☐ b. a wise precaution.
    - ☐ c. very important in cold climates.

33   Weight Control

We can help control weight by watching our food intake, the exercise we get, or both.

To keep the same weight, we must balance calories found in food and those used by the body. To lose weight, we must get fewer calories from food than the body uses. To gain weight, we must get more.

It takes about 3,500 extra calories to make a pound of stored fat. For each pound to be gained or lost, there must be 3,500 calories more or 3,500 calories less in the diet than the body uses.

If you plan to lose or gain weight by watching the amount of food eaten without changing activities, the rate of loss or gain will depend on the number of calories you subtract from or add to your diet each day.

For example, to lose two pounds a week a person would have to take in 7,000 calories fewer each week than the body uses. Or one would need 1,000 calories fewer each day. A person whose caloric need is 2,400 calories a day would cut down to 1,400 calories a day. It's a good idea not to go below 1,200 calories a day without a doctor's supervision because it is hard to get the minerals and vitamins we need from foods when diets have fewer calories than this.

The same figure—3,500 calories per pound of stored fat—can be used as a general guide in planning meals to add or maintain weight. However, the test of any of these figures for a person is his own weight record. There are so many differences in people, in food, and in the amount of energy used in carrying out activities that the figure may not be just right for you.

Because there is usually little change from day to day in the time spent at work and in daily living, leisure time probably offers the best chance for increased or decreased activity for weight control. Though this time may amount to only an hour or two a day, it can be used well.

Long hours spent in hard exercise are not necessary to keep weight under control. For many persons it is not recommended. Regular, less strenuous exercise can be effective for those who should take it easier, and who want to lose or maintain weight while eating enough food to be satisfied.

Recalling Facts

1. How many extra calories are needed to produce one pound of stored fat?
   - ☐ a. 1,500
   - ☐ b. 2,500
   - ☐ c. 3,500

2. A doctor should be consulted if daily calorie intake drops below
   - ☐ a. 1,200 calories.
   - ☐ b. 1,600 calories.
   - ☐ c. 2,000 calories.

3. The best opportunity for increasing exercise each day is
   - ☐ a. leisure time.
   - ☐ b. working time.
   - ☐ c. reading time.

4. Weight control is based on
   - ☐ a. heredity and luck.
   - ☐ b. food and activity.
   - ☐ c. hormones and fluids.

5. The author does not mention
   - ☐ a. which foods are fattening.
   - ☐ b. how to lose two pounds a week.
   - ☐ c. an individual's past weight record.

Understanding the Passage

6. The author states that one may lose weight most rapidly by
   - ☐ a. increasing exercise and decreasing food intake.
   - ☐ b. decreasing exercise and increasing food intake.
   - ☐ c. increasing exercise and increasing food intake.

7. For a person on a diet, a doctor would probably prescribe
   - ☐ a. extra sleep.
   - ☐ b. vitamin pills.
   - ☐ c. more water.

8. To keep weight under control, one should
   - ☐ a. exercise strenuously for several hours a day.
   - ☐ b. develop a regular schedule of exercise.
   - ☐ c. participate in several sports.

9. The author implies that weight control is
   - ☐ a. an exact science.
   - ☐ b. an area of great misunderstanding.
   - ☐ c. a matter of self-control.

10. The purpose of the selection is to
    - ☐ a. persuade the reader not to eat sweets.
    - ☐ b. identify the one cause of heart attacks.
    - ☐ c. prove that weight can be regulated.

34 Not a Drop to Drink

Not so long ago, most streams and lakes in America were sparkling and clean. People could swim and fish in them without becoming sick. But as the nation grew bigger, we built towns and factories on the banks of these streams and lakes. Every year we dumped more and more wastes into our waters. People thought that the water would carry the wastes away and purify itself. This was true when the amount of wastes was small. But as our population has grown, the greater amounts of wastes have not been well handled.

What we have done is to overload the water recycling system of the earth. Now most of our streams and lakes show signs of man's abuse. Many are very polluted. The Cuyahoga River in Ohio, for example, had so much rubble and oil in it that it actually caught fire several years ago.

One of our beautiful Great Lakes, Lake Erie, is in serious trouble as a result of aging. This is a natural process for all bodies of water, but it is speeded up by man's pollution. Certain pollutants make plants grow too fast and disturb the plant growth balance of the lake. Scientists say that pollution has aged Lake Erie many years in a very short time. To save it, we must stop dumping wastes into the lake and take strong action to clean it up.

Marine scientists have found that even the ocean depths show the effects of pollution. And in shallower waters near our coasts, pollution prevents the harvesting of fish and shellfish in many areas. Oil, spilled by accident or even dumped on purpose in the ocean, has become a big problem because it spoils our beaches and kills fish and sea birds.

The water that we drink is normally taken from the best and cleanest sources, then treated to make sure it is safe for drinking. But with so much pollution, it is harder to find good water. Even water far below the ground, from which many cities get their drinking water, is sometimes polluted by poisonous wastes flowing into the soil.

A shameful number of our planet's lakes, rivers, and even seas are being destroyed. A rapidly expanding world population and the growth of industry will cause the problem to get far worse in the years to come. Hence it is imperative that we build sewage treatment plants that can eliminate water pollution.

Recalling Facts

1. The river mentioned is located in
   - ☐ a. Texas.
   - ☐ b. Missouri.
   - ☐ c. Ohio.

2. The lake which is in serious trouble because of aging is
   - ☐ a. Lake Ontario.
   - ☐ b. Lake Erie.
   - ☐ c. Lake Michigan.

3. In order to protect waterways, it is imperative to
   - ☐ a. create large dams.
   - ☐ b. build more sewage treatment plants.
   - ☐ c. continue dumping sewage.

4. The author mentions one polluted river that
   - ☐ a. turned black.
   - ☐ b. caught fire.
   - ☐ c. caused disease.

5. Even below ground, water is sometimes
   - ☐ a. sparkling.
   - ☐ b. polluted.
   - ☐ c. black colored.

Understanding the Passage

6. This article is primarily about
   - ☐ a. waste systems used by industries.
   - ☐ b. the dangers of polluted water.
   - ☐ c. the work of marine scientists.

7. Not too long ago, people thought that pollutants in streams
   - ☐ a. were eventually carried out to sea.
   - ☐ b. dissolved when treated with detergents.
   - ☐ c. were absorbed by plants growing underwater.

8. The author is hopeful that
   - ☐ a. large companies will be fined for polluting streams.
   - ☐ b. communities will find sources of clean drinking water.
   - ☐ c. better sewage treatment plants will be built.

9. The author feels that pollution has become a serious problem because
   - ☐ a. the population has increased rapidly.
   - ☐ b. the government has been indifferent to the situation.
   - ☐ c. factories now use more chemicals than they once did.

10. We can conclude that
   - ☐ a. no clean water can be found anywhere.
   - ☐ b. pollution is difficult to control.
   - ☐ c. pollution laws are too strict.

Buying a Ladder

Ladders were once simple constructions of wood timbers and crosspieces, notched and bound with thongs. Today, the range of ladder designs, types, sizes, and materials is broad enough to meet all needs.

Before you make a trip to the store to buy a ladder, you should think about your needs. Will the ladder be used indoors or outdoors? How high will you want to climb? Who else will be using it? Where will it be stored?

If you live in an apartment, you will need a stepladder that will meet your needs and will be easy to handle. Its size will depend on the highest point you want to reach. You should remember that you must never stand on the top of a stepladder.

A person who lives in a house may need two ladders, a stepladder for indoor work and a straight ladder or extension ladder for use outdoors. The outdoor ladder should be long enough to extend a minimum of three feet higher than the highest area you want to reach.

A person who is buying a stepladder should never be hurried into making a quick purchase. The ladder should be checked for weak steps, loose rungs, or other defects before it is taken from the store.

A buyer should check to see if the name of the manufacturer or distributor appears on the label. This information may be important in case of a quality or accident problem.

Wood, aluminum, magnesium, and fiberglass are the principal materials used in the construction of modern ladders. Each type has its advantages and disadvantages.

Wood ladders are sturdy and bend little under loads for which they are designed. They are heavier than metal ladders, and large sizes are harder to handle. When dry, wood ladders are safe to use around electrical circuits or when a person is working with power tools.

Metal ladders are a little more expensive than wood ladders of the same quality. They last longer because they do not decay from moisture and sunlight and are not attacked by insects. Aluminum and magnesium ladders are light, weighing only about two-thirds as much as those made of wood.

Fiberglass is the newest material to appear on the ladder market. It is used to make the side rails of high-grade metal stepladders. The result is a ladder that is light, rust resistant, serviceable, and practically maintenance free.

---

*Reading Time*_____   *Comprehension Score*_____   *Words per Minute*_____

Recalling Facts

1. How far should outdoor ladders extend beyond the area to be reached?
   - ☐ a. one foot
   - ☐ b. two feet
   - ☐ c. three feet

2. The heaviest ladders are made of
   - ☐ a. fiberglass.
   - ☐ b. metal.
   - ☐ c. wood.

3. Ladders are sometimes made of a combination of fiberglass and
   - ☐ a. aluminum.
   - ☐ b. wood.
   - ☐ c. plastic.

4. What type of ladder is not affected by moisture and sunlight?
   - ☐ a. wood
   - ☐ b. aluminum
   - ☐ c. fiberglass

5. If a ladder proves to be defective, the buyer should contact the
   - ☐ a. police.
   - ☐ b. manufacturer.
   - ☐ c. Better Business Bureau.

Understanding the Passage

6. The author uses the word "thongs" to mean
   - ☐ a. special climbing shoes.
   - ☐ b. large support posts.
   - ☐ c. strips of leather.

7. The author implies that ladders should be
   - ☐ a. purchased carefully.
   - ☐ b. painted every year.
   - ☐ c. stored in a cool place.

8. The reader can assume that fiberglass is used
   - ☐ a. to make very long ladders.
   - ☐ b. to make the steps of ladders.
   - ☐ c. in stepladders.

9. The article suggests that
   - ☐ a. fiberglass ladders are more expensive than wood.
   - ☐ b. most people are afraid to climb ladders.
   - ☐ c. wooden ladders last longer than any other type.

10. This article is concerned with the
    - ☐ a. history of ladders.
    - ☐ b. selection of ladders.
    - ☐ c. manufacture of ladders.

The forty sightless youngsters came down from the bus, full of questions and wonder. Most of them knew little of what a hawk or an owl might look like—to say nothing of a goat, or an elephant, or a lamb.

A few of the children with some sight could see the outlines of an elephant or a donkey. But when it came to visiting a zoo, they, along with their totally blind friends, would use their hands and fingers to explore the forms of animal life. They would thus awaken in themselves the reality that comes from using the sense of touch.

Guides seated the youngsters in the zoo's theater. Then one of them named the animals they would "see," described their habits, and answered the questions that curious children have always asked: "Do owls sleep?" "Do hawks have teeth?" "Do apes make good mothers?"

Afterwards, other guides brought out stuffed owls and hawks, since live ones could not be handled, and let the young fingers discover shape and form. Their comments were mostly about the sense of touch: "Doesn't he feel funny?" "Watch out for that sharp beak!"

Later came the guinea pigs, turtles, and rabbits. They were a mixture of furs, feathers, shells, and hides, which delighted the group after they had overcome their doubts and first feelings about touching them.

Then they were led into the contact area where they found larger animals. Here they were allowed to feed carrots to the goats, pet the lambs and calves, and feel the wool and horns.

In the baby elephant area, one was reminded of the East Indian legend of the six blind men. Each of them felt some part of the elephant and came up with six different ideas of what kind of creature it really was.

The tail, trunk, and ears were touched and talked about while the calm little elephant stood still as if it knew that it was playing a part in an unusual learning process.

A half-serious moment developed when two youngsters, one on each side of the elephant, reached for the end of the trunk and accidentally touched hands underneath. "Aw, that's you!" said one of them laughingly. He realized that it was only the hand of his friend on the other side.

After two hours, the youngsters grew tired. This time of exploration and learning had been an adventure.

Recalling Facts

1. How many children visited the zoo?
   - □ a. ten
   - □ b. thirty
   - □ c. forty

2. The children were learning through
   - □ a. sight.
   - □ b. hearing.
   - □ c. touch.

3. The children visited the zoo's
   - □ a. theater.
   - □ b. bird house.
   - □ c. museum.

4. In the contact area the children found
   - □ a. small reptiles.
   - □ b. many geese.
   - □ c. larger animals.

5. A half-serious moment developed when two youngsters
   - □ a. angered a cow.
   - □ b. touched hands.
   - □ c. lost their lunch boxes.

Understanding the Passage

6. This article is concerned primarily with
   - □ a. the zoo experiences of inner city children.
   - □ b. a nature trail and zoo established for the blind.
   - □ c. "seeing" animals by touching them.

7. The author implies that
   - □ a. children are usually afraid of large animals.
   - □ b. hawks and owls are dangerous to handle.
   - □ c. elephants are often unpredictable.

8. The actions of the children suggest that they were
   - □ a. experienced with many kinds of animals.
   - □ b. hesitant about being with live animals.
   - □ c. difficult to control in the elephant compound.

9. The East Indian legend proves that
   - □ a. children are often awed by the wonders of nature.
   - □ b. elephants are difficult to identify without sight.
   - □ c. camels cannot go for long periods without water.

10. The children were curious about the
   - □ a. mothering instinct of apes.
   - □ b. reality of dragons.
   - □ c. blindness of bats.

Child Proofing

Poisonings that cause death happen most of the time to children between the ages of one and three. Some doctors call this stage the "Age of Accidents." Children want to look at things and taste them. They will eat or drink anything they can find, even if it tastes bad. You must make your home safe for children and protect them from poisoning.

Here are three things you can do. One, know which things around the home are poisons. Two, keep poisons out of your child's reach at all times. Three, be aware of how clever children are when it comes to finding poisons. ●

Nearly all chemicals and drugs in the home contain things that can poison someone. Be sure to read the labels on products you bring into the home. Look for the words which are meant as warnings. These warnings will read *Poison, Harmful if Swallowed, For External Use Only,* and *Keep Out of Reach of Children.* Look around your home for bottles and jars which bear these warnings. Then, put them away in a place where a child cannot reach or find them.

You should know that you cannot always rely on the label on a product ● to give you the proper warning. There are things such as nail polish, perfume, makeup, hair tonic, and others that give you no clue to the dangers that might result from swallowing. Drinks with alcohol, such as gin, whiskey, beer, and wine, do not carry warnings. These, too, can cause your child harm. You cannot know which of the hundreds of items are really dangerous. Therefore, your best line of defense is to suspect everything that is not a known and healthy food item.

A great number of plants, even those commonly found around the house, are poisonous. Teach your child never to eat any part of a plant unless it ● is served as food. This rule also applies to unknown berries and mushrooms. Even nibbling on leaves or sucking on plant stems is unsafe. Also, drinking water that plants have been soaking in can cause poisoning.

Some foods can be just as harmful as poisons when given to a child by mistake. For example, putting salt instead of sugar in baby's food can lead to illness. If you put sugar and salt into new jars, label them. Be sure to read the label each time before using.

If your child shows signs of poisoning, call your doctor right away.

Recalling Facts

1. Most child poisonings happen between the ages of
   - ☐ a. one and three.
   - ☐ b. four and six.
   - ☐ c. eight and ten.

2. Poisonous products should be
   - ☐ a. destroyed.
   - ☐ b. kept out of reach.
   - ☐ c. wrapped in newspaper.

3. Which of the following is a label warning?
   - ☐ a. Contents Under Pressure
   - ☐ b. For External Use Only
   - ☐ c. Nonaerosol Spray

4. A child can be poisoned by eating
   - ☐ a. too much food.
   - ☐ b. raw vegetables.
   - ☐ c. unknown berries.

5. What should you do if your child shows signs of poisoning?
   - ☐ a. Call your doctor.
   - ☐ b. Call your neighbor.
   - ☐ c. Wait 24 hours.

Understanding the Passage

6. What is this article about?
   - ☐ a. drug abuse and poison
   - ☐ b. household poisoning
   - ☐ c. poison control centers

7. Children often get into poisons because they
   - ☐ a. are curious.
   - ☐ b. are unsupervised.
   - ☐ c. want to help.

8. We can see that
   - ☐ a. most children will not drink something that tastes bad.
   - ☐ b. nearly all home products contain a harmful poison.
   - ☐ c. mushrooms and berries are good for children to eat.

9. The writer makes this article clear by using
   - ☐ a. facts.
   - ☐ b. opinions.
   - ☐ c. maps.

10. This article tells us that
    - ☐ a. doctors don't treat poison victims.
    - ☐ b. house plants give off oxygen.
    - ☐ c. too much salt can be harmful.

38 Civil Rights of Americans

All Americans have certain rights under the United States Constitution and federal laws. These rights protect you against unfair acts by government officials and private individuals.

It is up to you to use your rights. If you don't know what your rights are, ask for help from a lawyer. If you cannot pay a lawyer, one will be hired for you in most criminal cases. If you do not have a criminal case, you may be able to get help from a legal assistance program. You can find a legal assistance program by looking in your phone book or by calling the local bar (lawyers') association.

You have the right to believe what you wish and to state your beliefs in speech or in print. The rights to free speech and press are protected by the first amendment to the United States Constitution.

No government official at the federal, state, or local level can punish you for your beliefs or for stating them to others. You have the right to freely join together with others in social, political, or religious groups, such as political parties and churches. The government can make rules about when, where, and how you or your group may speak out in public, but these rules must be reasonable.

The federal and state governments cannot favor any one religious group over another. They cannot cut off any government services because you say what your beliefs are. You are free to choose your own religion or faith. Or, if you want to, you can decide not to have any religious belief at all.

An important right is your right to "petition for a redress of grievance." What this means is that you can freely tell your government officials about any problems that bother you.

Adult citizens have the right to register to vote, join political parties, and vote. They can run for office in all elections on the federal, state, and local levels. No one can charge you a fee, make you pay a poll tax, make you take a literacy test or make you speak or read English in order to vote. Elections must be held fairly, and all votes must be counted equally. If someone threatens you or tries to take away your rights to register and vote, report it to the Assistant Attorney General, Civil Rights Division, Department of Justice, Washington, D.C.

Recalling Facts

1. The article says that to learn what your rights are, ask a
   □ a. lawyer.
   □ b. congressman.
   □ c. state official.

2. Which amendment protects a person's rights to free speech?
   □ a. first
   □ b. fifth
   □ c. tenth

3. The document which gives Americans certain rights is the
   □ a. Declaration of Independence.
   □ b. Constitution.
   □ c. Rights of Redress.

4. A bar association is a group of
   □ a. lawyers.
   □ b. judges.
   □ c. city officials.

5. If someone stops you from voting, you can report it to the Department of
   □ a. Defense.
   □ b. Justice.
   □ c. State.

Understanding the Passage

6. This selection is mostly about
   □ a. United States documents.
   □ b. legal restrictions on Americans.
   □ c. civil rights for Americans.

7. If you are unable to pay a private lawyer's fees, the
   □ a. court will provide a lawyer free of charge.
   □ b. lawyer will offer reduced fees to meet your ability.
   □ c. court may refuse to hear your case temporarily.

8. In regard to speaking out in public, the government may
   □ a. tell you that you cannot speak in certain places.
   □ b. prohibit you from speaking against certain politicians.
   □ c. arrest you for publicly approving of foreign governments.

9. Under a "petition for a redress of grievance," you should
   □ a. write to a lawyer for assistance.
   □ b. contact your state senator.
   □ c. demand that you be heard in the Court of Appeals.

10. In order to vote in any election, you must know
    □ a. how to pay a poll tax.
    □ b. when an election is being held.
    □ c. where an intelligence test is being given.

A Living Link

In a land with a history as long as Britain's, the past is an important part of the people's way of life. The Royal Family is a living link with the kings and the tales of the past. To the British, Queen Elizabeth II is a symbol of Britain's unity. Wherever and whenever she appears, she is given respect and warm feelings.

Many of the old customs that are part of this respect for the Royal Family are still followed today.

Even in this modern age the Monarch's Champion can be seen in the parade held when a new ruler takes the throne. The Champion's role now is to carry the royal flag. Up until 200 years ago, the knight who had this title rode his horse into the banquet hall where the new king was dining. There he shouted out a challenge to fight anyone who did not believe that the new king was the rightful heir to the throne.

In late October or early November the Queen personally takes part in another old and colorful ceremony. This is the Opening of Parliament. From Buckingham Palace to the Parliament, thousands of Britons line the streets to see their ruler pass in a horse-drawn carriage.

Another old ceremony, Trooping the Colour, takes place in London in early June. It is also called the Queen's Birthday Parade since it marks the official birthday of the ruler. This is an important military event. It is a time when the Queen inspects units of the Brigade of Guards.

Some of the British customs are not related to the life of the Royal Family.

A yearly event with an old beginning is Guy Fawkes Day, November 5. This marks the day in 1605 on which Fawkes tried to blow up the Parliament buildings. Now, weeks before the event, in every part of the United Kingdom children carry a homemade, stuffed likeness of Fawkes and ask for "a penny for the Guy." The money they collect is spent on fireworks and candy.

Only a few days later is the City of London's finest show. This is the day when the elected Lord Mayor of the City of London takes office. For the event the Lord Mayor is carried from the Guildhall to the law courts in a horse-drawn coach. There he is met by an agent of the ruler and his election is made official.

Recalling Facts

1. To the British, Queen Elizabeth represents
   - ☐ a. justice.
   - ☐ b. courage.
   - ☐ c. unity.

2. The role of the Monarch's Champion is to carry a
   - ☐ a. flag.
   - ☐ b. crown.
   - ☐ c. sword.

3. The Opening of Parliament occurs in the
   - ☐ a. spring.
   - ☐ b. summer.
   - ☐ c. fall.

4. Guy Fawkes became famous during the early
   - ☐ a. 1500s.
   - ☐ b. 1600s.
   - ☐ c. 1700s.

5. The Queen inspects units of the Brigade of Guards
   - ☐ a. during the Queen's Birthday Parade.
   - ☐ b. on Guy Fawkes Day.
   - ☐ c. during the Opening of Parliament.

Understanding the Passage

6. The original role of the Monarch's Champion was to
   - ☐ a. slay the enemy in combat.
   - ☐ b. defend the rights of the king.
   - ☐ c. predict the future for royalty.

7. The title, "A Living Link," refers to
   - ☐ a. the continuation of the Royal Family.
   - ☐ b. scientific discoveries in the origins of man.
   - ☐ c. Great Britain's geological history.

8. In English history Guy Fawkes was a
   - ☐ a. hero.
   - ☐ b. criminal.
   - ☐ c. member of royalty.

9. Guy Fawkes Day is most similar to the American
   - ☐ a. Christmas.
   - ☐ b. Thanksgiving.
   - ☐ c. Halloween.

10. The Lord Mayor of London
    - ☐ a. is the most powerful figure in England.
    - ☐ b. is always related to the Royal Family.
    - ☐ c. takes office in November.

40   Man Overboard!

The careful boatman would be wise to take a tip from experienced sea-going men who know the value of being prepared for emergencies. A person going boating in a large or a small craft should think out plans that he would follow in emergencies. In this way his actions will be automatic, fast, and correct.

One problem that should be thought out beforehand is a time when a man is overboard. If a man is overboard, swing the stern of the boat away from him. This action will reduce the propeller danger to the man overboard.

Throw a lifesaving device to him as soon as possible, even if he can swim. Care should be taken not to hit the man. Normally, a life ring is the best lifesaving device to use for this purpose because it can be thrown farther and is easier for the man in the water to use. Don't wait to get a life ring if there is another lifesaving device closer at hand. Speed may be most important.

Keep the man in view at all times. If you have another person in the boat with you, have him act as lookout. If it is night, direct the brightest light on the man in the water. The way that you approach a man in the water depends upon common sense and good judgment. Consider the temperature of the water, the sea conditions, the physical condition and ability of the man in the water, and whether or not you are alone in the boat.

If you have someone in the boat with you, it might be a good idea to have this person put on a life preserver with a line attached to the boat and get into the water to help the person who fell overboard.

Help the man in boarding the boat. It is often difficult to climb into a boat from the water. And if a man is hurt or cold he may not be able to pull himself in. In small boats the weight of man suspended from the side might be enough to tip the boat and cause it to take in water. The best place for coming aboard a small boat would be by way of the stern or bow. Common sense says that the propeller should be stopped when taking a man over the stern.

Recalling Facts

1. Which part of a boat should be turned away from a person overboard?
   - ☐ a. the stern
   - ☐ b. the bow
   - ☐ c. the port side

2. The best lifesaving device for a person in the water is a
   - ☐ a. life jacket.
   - ☐ b. piece of wood.
   - ☐ c. life ring.

3. One factor to consider in a rescue operation is
   - ☐ a. wind direction.
   - ☐ b. water temperature.
   - ☐ c. weather forecast.

4. A rescued man should be taken aboard a small boat by way of the
   - ☐ a. stern or bow.
   - ☐ b. starboard side.
   - ☐ c. port side.

5. In this article, the author mentions
   - ☐ a. the Coast Guard.
   - ☐ b. boat fires.
   - ☐ c. sea conditions.

Understanding the Passage

6. This article could have been titled
   - ☐ a. Sinking Ships.
   - ☐ b. Be Prepared.
   - ☐ c. Lifesaving Devices.

7. The content of this selection is based upon
   - ☐ a. little-known facts about the sea.
   - ☐ b. friendly advice for the reader.
   - ☐ c. several interesting sea stories.

8. The author implies that
   - ☐ a. cold water is an obstacle to rescue operations.
   - ☐ b. a boat should move with the wind during a rescue.
   - ☐ c. small boats are more stable than larger boats.

9. It is sometimes advisable to
   - ☐ a. call the nearest Coast Guard station for assistance.
   - ☐ b. have an assistant swim to the man overboard.
   - ☐ c. measure the depth of the water at the time of rescue.

10. A person must be in good physical condition to
    - ☐ a. operate a small boat successfully.
    - ☐ b. supervise rescue operations.
    - ☐ c. endure rough seas while awaiting rescue.

41 A Free Woman

Thirty years ago, the worst that was said was "nice girls don't smoke" or "it'll stunt your growth."

Even years later when the Surgeon General's report showed the connection between smoking and lung cancer and other diseases, the facts were only about men. But now reports show that women who smoke are dying of lung cancer and other diseases at twice the rate of women who don't. Women who smoke are sick more often than women who don't. Women who smoke heavily have three times as much bronchitis or emphysema and 50 percent more peptic ulcers. Smoking even affects pregnancy. So you don't have to wait until you're old to feel the effects of smoking. If you're pregnant and you smoke, it can harm the health of your baby.

What happens when you smoke a cigarette?

In just three seconds a cigarette makes your heart beat faster and shoots your blood pressure up. It replaces oxygen in your blood with carbon monoxide and leaves cancer-causing chemicals to spread through your body. As the cigarettes add up, the damage adds up. It's the total amount of smoking that causes the trouble. The younger you start smoking, the greater your danger will be. For instance, if you're fifteen, you will have smoked many more cigarettes by the time you're thirty than someone who started at twenty.

And people who start young tend to become heavy smokers. Heavy smokers run a greater risk. Again, the more cigarettes you smoke, the faster they add up.

You're still young. The younger you are, the easier it is to quit. It takes years to develop a real cigarette habit. So even if you think you're hooked, chances are you're not. If you quit now, you will never be sorry. Your body will repair itself. Food will taste better. Everything will smell better (including your hair and your clothes). And don't let anyone tell you stories about gaining weight. Haven't you ever seen a fat smoker? If you have the willpower to quit smoking, you have the willpower not to overeat. It is as simple as that. You know what you've got to look forward to. You can grow into a truly free woman, or you can ruin yourself for life.

To smoke or not to smoke—that is the question. The only one who can make the choice is you.

Recalling Facts

1. The connection between smoking and cancer was made by
   - ☐ a. the A.M.A.
   - ☐ b. the government doctors.
   - ☐ c. the Surgeon General.

2. Smoking can increase a person's chances of developing
   - ☐ a. liver disease.
   - ☐ b. ulcers.
   - ☐ c. weight problems.

3. Smoking makes the heart beat faster after a lapse of
   - ☐ a. three seconds.
   - ☐ b. ten seconds.
   - ☐ c. twenty seconds.

4. According to the article, smoking
   - ☐ a. causes dizziness.
   - ☐ b. kills red blood cells.
   - ☐ c. raises blood pressure.

5. The author points out that giving up smoking requires
   - ☐ a. courage.
   - ☐ b. patience.
   - ☐ c. willpower.

Understanding the Passage

6. This article is mostly about
   - ☐ a. giving up smoking.
   - ☐ b. attitudes toward smoking.
   - ☐ c. the connection between growing and smoking.

7. The author implies that a person who gives up smoking
   - ☐ a. gains weight.
   - ☐ b. enjoys food more.
   - ☐ c. sleeps more soundly.

8. The reader can infer that
   - ☐ a. smoking can cause the common cold.
   - ☐ b. the odor of smoke clings to cloth.
   - ☐ c. cigarettes are more popular than cigars and pipes.

9. Giving up smoking is easiest for someone who is
   - ☐ a. twenty years old.
   - ☐ b. forty years old.
   - ☐ c. sixty years old.

10. The reader can conclude that
    - ☐ a. cigarette sales have declined in the past few years.
    - ☐ b. illnesses and smoking are often related.
    - ☐ c. cancer kills more people than any other disease.

All humans needs protein. It is the body's main tissue builder. It is the basic substance of every cell in the body. Protein's many functions include helping to make hemoglobin. This is the blood protein that carries oxygen to the cells and carries carbon dioxide away from them. Protein also helps to form antibodies that fight infection and it supplies energy.

The proteins in food are made up of eighteen or more amino acids. The body can make its own supply of more than half of these. But the others must come from food and are called essential amino acids. After foods are eaten, the proteins are broken down into amino acids. They are then re-arranged to form the many special proteins in the body.

The amount of amino acid in a food protein shows its nutritive value. Proteins that supply all the essential amino acids are highest in value. Foods that contain large amounts of these good proteins best meet the body's needs. Generally, these are foods from animals like meat, fish, poultry, eggs, and milk.

Proteins from cereal grains, vegetables, and fruits do not have as many kinds of amino acids as animal proteins do, but they do supply valuable amounts of many amino acids. Proteins from legumes, especially soybeans, chickpeas, and peanuts, are almost as good as proteins from animal sources.

Large amounts of protein are found in meat, fish, milk, cheese, eggs, dry beans, dry peas, and nuts. Bread, cereals, vegetables, and fruits have smaller amounts of protein. Eating the proper balance from the four main food groups will assure you of getting enough protein in your diet.

Including protein in each meal is important. To have daily meals rank well in protein quality, only a part of the protein has to come from animal sources. Combining cereals and vegetables with a little meat or other source of animal protein will improve the protein value of the meal. Examples of nourishing combinations are cereal with milk, rice with fish, spaghetti with meat sauce, or vegetable stew with meat. Milk along with foods of plant origin is also nourishing.

It is not always necessary to eat animal protein to have the proper amounts of protein in your diet. Vegetarians have developed ways of combining certain foods to make a complete protein. It is important, however, to learn which foods to combine in order to get good amounts of protein.

Recalling Facts

1. How many amino acids do proteins contain?
   - □ a. nine
   - □ b. thirteen
   - □ c. eighteen

2. Essential amino acids come from
   - □ a. food.
   - □ b. the body.
   - □ c. vitamins.

3. The highest amounts of amino acids are found in
   - □ a. vegetables.
   - □ b. cereal grains.
   - □ c. poultry.

4. According to the author, protein helps people to
   - □ a. relax.
   - □ b. fight infection.
   - □ c. think.

5. The nutritive value of food proteins is determined by
   - □ a. calories.
   - □ b. amino acids.
   - □ c. metabolism.

Understanding the Passage

6. The author suggests that
   - □ a. the body can manufacture at least nine amino acids.
   - □ b. sugar does not contain any protein.
   - □ c. some people are unable to absorb protein.

7. In this article, the author stresses the need for
   - □ a. having a high-protein breakfast each day.
   - □ b. eating protein at each meal.
   - □ c. always substituting vegetable protein for meat protein.

8. The author mentions a meal of spaghetti with meat sauce as
   - □ a. an example of a poorly balanced meal.
   - □ b. an illustration of a meal high in starch.
   - □ c. a sample of a nourishing meal.

9. This article is probably from a
   - □ a. scientific article on the structure of protein.
   - □ b. magazine on nutrition.
   - □ c. technical journal on body chemistry.

10. We can conclude that
    - □ a. vegetarians are basically unhealthy people.
    - □ b. some foods are richer sources of protein than others.
    - □ c. children need more protein than adults.

43 Wild Horses

The capture and taming of wild horses has long been a classic theme of American literature.

It is hard to say just when the local ranchers stopped thinking of the wild horse as an asset and started to consider it a pest. The change in attitude was probably tied to many things.

The population of the West had increased, and open land had started to fill up. With the coming of the automobile and the tractor, the value and usefulness of the horse decreased. In some places the wild horse became a serious competitor with domestic livestock for forage. For these and other reasons the rancher's way of looking at the wild horse changed, and between 1920 and 1960 many ranchers would shoot a wild horse on sight.

Then, during this period, another factor was added. The wild horse became an economic asset—but only after it was dead. In an affluent era, more people started to buy canned food for their pets. To meet the demand, enterprising people set up plants to process horseflesh. It became profitable to hunt, capture, and deliver wild horses to the canneries. The wild horse was then the prey of the commercial hunter.

Within a few years, the commercial hunter did what the rancher with his rifle had not been able to do. He seriously depleted the ranks of the wild herds in every state having open range.

The commercial hunter brought modern technology to the business of rounding up wild horses. The wild horse was wily and tough and knew the lay of the land. It could often outrun and outmaneuver a man on horseback, but it was not a match for motor vehicles. The commercial hunter brought in airplanes to flush the animals out of rough country and trucks or pickups to run the animals down once they were in the open. After a horse was roped, a weight was tied to the free end of the lariat, and the animal was left to wear itself out as it dragged the weight and fought the unfamiliar rope. When exhausted, the horse was loaded into a truck and hauled to the processing plant.

Commercial hunters were paid by the pound, and they had to deliver many pounds of flesh to make a living. Few felt that they could afford the extra time required to handle the animals in a humane manner.

Recalling Facts

1. The wild horse became the prey of the commercial hunter for its
   - ☐ a. meat.
   - ☐ b. hide.
   - ☐ c. hair.

2. According to the author, ranchers were never able to control
   - ☐ a. horse migrations.
   - ☐ b. horse populations.
   - ☐ c. commercial hunting.

3. Horses were rounded up by using
   - ☐ a. dogs.
   - ☐ b. guns.
   - ☐ c. planes.

4. When horses were taken to the processing plants, they were
   - ☐ a. exhausted.
   - ☐ b. dying.
   - ☐ c. dead.

5. Commercial hunters were paid by the
   - ☐ a. pound.
   - ☐ b. horse.
   - ☐ c. truckload.

Understanding the Passage

6. Hunters found that wild horses were
   - ☐ a. cunning.
   - ☐ b. lazy.
   - ☐ c. dangerous.

7. Many commercial hunters
   - ☐ a. were being cruel in their hunting methods.
   - ☐ b. thought processing plants should be outlawed.
   - ☐ c. restricted the killing of horses.

8. The author implies that
   - ☐ a. hunters were pressured to kill many animals.
   - ☐ b. ranchers did not approve of commerical horse hunting.
   - ☐ c. horses breed faster than other grazing animals.

9. The year 1920 marks the turning point in
   - ☐ a. methods used to capture wild horses.
   - ☐ b. ranchers' attitudes toward wild horses.
   - ☐ c. the condition of grazing lands.

10. The work of the commercial hunter is described as
    - ☐ a. an ingenious experiment.
    - ☐ b. a scarcely profitable enterprise.
    - ☐ c. a sophisticated operation.

44   Think Before You Buy

Before you shop for a carpet for your home, think about colors and textures. What will look good in your home? How long will the carpeting keep its pleasing appearance?

Red, orange, and yellow are warm colors. They tend to create a lively and cheery feeling. They are good in rooms that get little sunlight. Also, they can make a large room seem cozier. In a small room, though, they can be overpowering.

Green, blue, and violet are cool colors. These colors are useful for sunny rooms or for a formal setting. They tend to make rooms seem cooler and larger.

Gray and beige are neutral. They go well with either warm or cool colors. Neutral colors will blend well with colors already in a room. No matter what color carpet you choose, it will look better in your room if it is part of a planned color scheme.

Single-color schemes are made up of various shades of one color, ranging from light to dark. Use the darkest shade in the carpet and lighter shades in curtains or furniture. Examples of a contrasting-color scheme would be orange with green or blue with yellow. Make one color stand out and have only small things in the contrasting color. If the carpet color contrasts with the walls, the effect will clash too much. Use the contrasting color instead in upholstery fabrics.

Texture is important, too. Smooth, even surface textures made of long, closely packed yarns give carpets an expensive look. An uneven texture gives a less formal effect. Patterns or designs can highlight either one of these effects.

Light carpet colors show soil and dust easily. They should not be used if your home has forced-air heat. Air-borne dust will soon darken light colors around air vents. Black, dark brown, and other deep colors show lint. A mixture of two or more colors, patterns, and designs tends to hide soil. Multi-colored rugs are a wise choice if you don't want your carpet to show the dirt.

Also, even textures tend to show dirt and dust more than uneven textures. Uneven textures, however, are harder to clean and may need more strokes of a vacuum cleaner.

The next time you are in the market for a good carpet, keep these few simple facts in mind. Take time to think about your choice—it will make a world of difference.

Recalling Facts

1. When you choose a carpet for your home, you should think about the rug's color and
   □ a. price.
   □ b. texture.
   □ c. weight.

2. Red, orange, and yellow are
   □ a. cool colors.
   □ b. sad colors.
   □ c. warm colors.

3. Green, blue, and violet go well in
   □ a. a dark room.
   □ b. a formal setting.
   □ c. an informal setting.

4. Neutral colors are
   □ a. gray and beige.
   □ b. green and blue.
   □ c. red and yellow.

5. Light carpet colors should not be used in a home that has
   □ a. air conditioning.
   □ b. forced-air heat.
   □ c. steam radiators.

Understanding the Passage

6. Red, orange, and yellow color schemes can make you feel
   □ a. cold.
   □ b. cozy.
   □ c. sad.

7. What colors are best in a small room?
   □ a. red, orange, and yellow
   □ b. green, blue, and violet
   □ c. white, black, and gray

8. A room decorated in orange and black is an example of a
   □ a. contrasting-color scheme.
   □ b. multi-color scheme.
   □ c. single-color scheme.

9. A carpet with long, closely packed yarns would probably feel
   □ a. coarse.
   □ b. thick.
   □ c. thin.

10. Uneven-textured carpets
    □ a. are easy to clean.
    □ b. do not show the dirt.
    □ c. will not fade or shrink.

45 The Kennedy Half Dollar

The Kennedy half dollar was first made in 1964 as a tribute to the late president.

John Fitzgerald Kennedy, 35th president of the United States, is remembered as an active and eager president. He entered the White House in 1961 at the age of 43, one of our youngest presidents. Even by then, he had lived a full and colorful life. After graduation from Harvard College, he toured Europe and visited Great Britain. In the same year, he published his first book, *Why England Slept,* a study of pre-World War II British politics.

As a junior navy lieutenant during World War II, he commanded a PT boat in the Pacific. His boat was hit by a Japanese destroyer. The collision dumped the crew of twelve men into the ocean in the middle of flaming gasoline. Kennedy swam to a nearby island with the rest of his crew. He towed a wounded crewman by a life jacket that he gripped in his teeth. This swim took five hours. It won him the Navy and Marine Corps Medal for courage and bravery.

Kennedy's youth and spirit captured the hearts of the American people. His speeches were not only words, but calls to duty and action. He led the nation to a new belief in the freedoms of America. He called upon people to meet the demands of a new age of our country and for the whole free world.

Kennedy's dream for America went into the homes and shops of cities around the world. People began to look to America with new hopes. His life was cut short by a sniper's bullet on November 23, 1963, as he rode in a motorcade through downtown Dallas, Texas. He had been President for less than three years. The nation was plunged into grief as he was laid to rest in Arlington National Cemetery.

The back of the Kennedy half dollar bears the Presidential Coat of Arms. It features the American spread eagle holding the olive branch of peace in one claw and a bundle of arrows meaning defense in the other. The Presidential Seal was first used about 1878. It was probably taken from the Great Seal of the United States. According to custom, the eagle faces to the left toward the bundle of arrows during wartime. It faces to the right toward honor and the olive branches in peacetime.

Recalling Facts

1. The Kennedy half dollar was first issued in
   □ a. 1964.
   □ b. 1966.
   □ c. 1968.

2. Kennedy became president at the age of
   □ a. 38.
   □ b. 43.
   □ c. 47.

3. At one time, Kennedy commanded a PT boat in the
   □ a. Atlantic.
   □ b. Pacific.
   □ c. Mediterranean.

4. Kennedy was president for less than
   □ a. one year.
   □ b. two years.
   □ c. three years.

5. After graduation from college, Kennedy visited
   □ a. Great Britain.
   □ b. Mexico.
   □ c. Russia.

Understanding the Passage

6. The author offers proof that Kennedy was
   □ a. heroic.
   □ b. sincere.
   □ c. hardworking.

7. According to the author, Kennedy's speeches
   □ a. helped to improve relations between America and Russia.
   □ b. aroused interest in the space program.
   □ c. gave Americans new hope for the country.

8. The author concludes the article with a discussion of
   □ a. Kennedy's naval career.
   □ b. Kennedy's death and funeral.
   □ c. the Kennedy half dollar.

9. Before he became president, Kennedy
   □ a. wrote a book about England.
   □ b. was the American ambassador to England.
   □ c. lived in England for several years.

10. Kennedy thought that the world was
    □ a. entering a new age.
    □ b. heading toward nuclear war.
    □ c. falling into the grips of inflation.

Democracy is a way of life. Like other living things, it needs care. To keep democracy alive in the United States, every citizen must do his share to protect it. Voting in elections is one of the important ways of protecting democracy. When they vote, the citizens help express the will of the people. It is not only the right of every American citizen to vote, but it is also his responsibility.

Voting, in itself, is not enough. If we are to have leaders who will give us good government, we must choose them wisely. Every voter should learn all he can about the candidates and the issues in an election. He should know why he is for or against a candidate or an issue.

A good citizen does not vote one way or another just to please a friend or neighbor. The intelligent voter thinks for himself and makes his own decisions. His vote is secret.

There are many ways that a voter can learn about the candidates and the issues. He can listen to persons who are helping the candidate to win the election. These people tell what the candidate promises to do for the citizens if they elect him. The voter can also attend meetings and hear the candidate himself. Information about candidates and issues is given in newspapers, magazines, and books. Circulars and pamphlets sent to the homes of voters by political parties are other sources of information.

The intelligent voter can also get information in his own home. Members of the family can talk about what they think. The same thing can be done at the place where the voter works.

The voter should learn what is said for each candidate and issue, as well as what is said against them. It would be foolish for him to believe every-thing that he hears and reads. By learning about each side, the voter can compare the information and then make up his own mind. This is the intelligent way of keeping democracy alive.

The duty of a good citizen does not end with voting. After the election is over, a voter should make sure that the person who was elected is doing what he promised he would do. He may not be keeping his promises. When this happens, the voters have a duty to elect a better person at the next election.

Recalling Facts

1. The author describes democracy as
   - ☐ a. the oldest form of government.
   - ☐ b. a blessing for the poor.
   - ☐ c. a living thing.

2. One way to protect democracy is to
   - ☐ a. hold office.
   - ☐ b. vote.
   - ☐ c. save money.

3. The author does not mention advertising
   - ☐ a. on television.
   - ☐ b. in newspapers.
   - ☐ c. in books.

4. A good citizen votes in elections to please
   - ☐ a. his family.
   - ☐ b. his friends.
   - ☐ c. himself.

5. The author feels that members of a family should
   - ☐ a. vote differently.
   - ☐ b. discuss candidates.
   - ☐ c. avoid discussing politics.

Understanding the Passage

6. According to the author, people should vote for
   - ☐ a. friends and relatives.
   - ☐ b. people whom they have met personally.
   - ☐ c. people who are most qualified.

7. People who help candidates to win elections usually
   - ☐ a. provide important information for voters.
   - ☐ b. make false and misleading statements.
   - ☐ c. cause candidates to lose many friends.

8. The author states that some political parties
   - ☐ a. send pamphlets.
   - ☐ b. debate in public.
   - ☐ c. spend money foolishly.

9. The author advises the voter to
   - ☐ a. keep his views a secret.
   - ☐ b. discuss political issues at work.
   - ☐ c. campaign for at least one politician.

10. We can conclude that
    - ☐ a. an informed citizen is an intelligent voter.
    - ☐ b. most people vote without knowing the issues.
    - ☐ c. some politicians are elected by mistake.

47 The Land of Bagpipes

Scotland is in the northern part of Great Britain. The Scots are a proud people. They are especially proud of their fighting skills. They claim theirs is the only country in Europe that has never been conquered.

As one travels north, the climate begins to turn colder. That is, colder for visitors, but "just brisk" to the Scots.

Some of the world's finest tweeds come from the cities and towns around the River Tweed in the section of Scotland closest to England. And since almost every part of the country touches the sea, some of the best fish dishes are served in restaurants and hotels.

Most visitors to Scotland start with the capital city of Edinburgh. Almost as soon as they arrive, they know that this is Robert Burns's country since his monument can be seen in the center of the city.

Only a short journey away is Linlithgow Castle where Mary Stuart, Queen of Scots, was born in 1542. Edinburgh Castle is another sight sure to be pointed out to visitors.

On a clear day one has a good view of the city from the castle. Jewels and crowns of ancient Scottish rulers are displayed inside.

Only a short journey away is the city of Glasgow on the Clyde River. While many visitors explore this modern city, most head on steamers for the island resorts that are found in the area.

Scotland is the home of golf and there are excellent courses at St. Andrews. While this ancient town is best known to foreign visitors for its courses, it is also the site of St. Andrews University, the oldest institution of higher learning in Scotland. Famed for its ghosts, Glamis Castle can be visited on the way to see Balmoral Castle, the Highland residence of the Royal Family. The sound of bagpipes can be heard when the Queen is in residence.

As one goes farther north, Scotland becomes more mountainous. Flocks of sheep can be seen on the hillsides and the Loch Ness monster is also spotted once in a while. Many claim to have seen the monster after making one or more stops to sample the whisky for which Scotland is known.

Loch Lomond has no monster to attract visitors but it is located in one of the prettiest areas of Scotland. Each year it draws thousands of hikers. Hiking is a popular way to see the countryside.

Recalling Facts

1. Scotland is located in
   - ☐ a. northern Great Britain.
   - ☐ b. western Great Britain.
   - ☐ c. eastern Great Britain.

2. The author mentions that the Scots are
   - ☐ a. skillful.
   - ☐ b. proud.
   - ☐ c. clever.

3. Scotland is famous for its
   - ☐ a. tweeds.
   - ☐ b. flowers.
   - ☐ c. cheeses.

4. People travel to St. Andrews to play
   - ☐ a. tennis.
   - ☐ b. cricket.
   - ☐ c. golf.

5. Scotland raises many
   - ☐ a. sheep.
   - ☐ b. cows.
   - ☐ c. pigs.

Understanding the Passage

6. The article suggests that Scotland shares a border with
   - ☐ a. Ireland.
   - ☐ b. Wales.
   - ☐ c. England.

7. The Scots claim that
   - ☐ a. England does not give them enough freedom in government.
   - ☐ b. Ireland is unfriendly toward them.
   - ☐ c. Scotland has never been conquered in war.

8. The reader can infer that
   - ☐ a. Scotland has a long shoreline.
   - ☐ b. England is very cold during the summer months.
   - ☐ c. Wales is west of England.

9. Bagpipes are played in Scotland when
   - ☐ a. a famous artist dies.
   - ☐ b. the queen visits the area.
   - ☐ c. a storm is expected.

10. The author suggests that the Loch Ness monster
    - ☐ a. is a danger to local residents.
    - ☐ b. should be captured.
    - ☐ c. does not really exist.

Hiking is not only one of the best forms of physical exercise, but it is also one of the best forms of mental diversion. It is both relaxing and stimulating. It is good for all ages and especially good as a family and group activity.

Since hiking varies so widely in the distances covered and the types of trails and terrains, it is not possible to give any general rules to follow. Short and frequent hikes, needing no planning or special equipment, are enjoyed by most people.

• Keep in shape by walking at a fast pace for at least 15 minutes every day. Climbing stairs instead of using an elevator and running short distances are also good ways of keeping in shape.

• Wear only comfortable clothing. And when you are hiking in the mountains or in areas subject to sudden changes in the weather, take a windbreaker, a sweater, or other protection against cold and rain. Two pairs of socks, one thin and one thick, should be worn on long hikes.

• On any hike nothing is more important than good, comfortable shoes.

• The things you take might include matches in a waterproof box, a knife, compass, map, bandages and other first aid items, insect repellent, and a flashlight.

• Food can vary from a box of raisins on a short hike to dehydrated meals cooked over a small stove during a long hike.

• Binoculars or cameras may be taken, but don't overload with too much gear.

• On longer hikes keep a comfortable, steady pace and take rest stops often.

• Drink only safe water. If in doubt, boil the water or use purification tablets.

• Avoid the busy roads. When you have to use a road, keep as far over on the left as possible.

• Leave word at home or some other place as to where you are going and when you plan to return.

• On almost any hike, a map is a good idea. If going into strange country, a detailed map showing contours and landmarks is most helpful.

• Take along a field guide on flowers, birds, rocks, or other subjects depending upon your interests. This can add greatly to the enjoyment and educational value of your hike.

Much of the most beautiful scenery lies hidden away from the main roads. How much more fun it is to get out of your car and enjoy the fun and exercise of a hike in the outdoors!

Recalling Facts

1. The author recommends keeping in shape with a daily walk of
   - ☐ a. 15 minutes.
   - ☐ b. 30 minutes.
   - ☐ c. 45 minutes.

2. The author feels that the most essential item on a hike is
   - ☐ a. a new map.
   - ☐ b. outdoor tools.
   - ☐ c. good shoes.

3. A good snack for a short hike would be
   - ☐ a. beans.
   - ☐ b. crackers.
   - ☐ c. raisins.

4. When you walk on a highway, keep to the
   - ☐ a. right.
   - ☐ b. left.
   - ☐ c. middle.

5. The author mentions that hiking is especially valuable for
   - ☐ a. individuals.
   - ☐ b. families.
   - ☐ c. retirees.

Understanding the Passage

6. This article is about hiking as a
   - ☐ a. competitive sport.
   - ☐ b. leisurely pastime.
   - ☐ c. strenuous activity.

7. The article implies that hiking is
   - ☐ a. a relaxing form of exercise.
   - ☐ b. a dangerous activity for older people.
   - ☐ c. not as popular as it was once.

8. The author of this selection is mostly concerned with
   - ☐ a. general rules for hiking in mountainous areas.
   - ☐ b. precautions to be taken against dangerous animals.
   - ☐ c. general procedures to follow in hiking.

9. The author recommends
   - ☐ a. leaving binoculars and cameras at home.
   - ☐ b. drinking water from streams only.
   - ☐ c. avoiding highways.

10. To develop the main idea the author uses
    - ☐ a. arguments.
    - ☐ b. suggestions.
    - ☐ c. comparisons.

The Bean Pot

Beans are among the oldest of foods and today are considered an important staple for millions of people.

They were once considered to be worth their weight in gold. The jeweler's "carat" owes its origin to a pealike bean on the east coast of Africa.

Beans also once figured very prominently in politics. During the age of the Romans, balloting was done with beans. White beans represented a vote of approval and dark beans meant a negative vote. Today, beans still play an active role in politics. Bean soup is a daily "must" in both the Senate and the House dining rooms in the nation's capital.

Beans undergo rather extensive processing before reaching the consumer. They are delivered to huge processing plants where they are cleaned to remove pods, stems, and other debris. Special machines separate debris by weight and then screen the beans by size. Discolored beans are removed by machines equipped with photosensitive electric eyes.

Many varieties of beans may be found on the grocery shelf. Although a shopper will not find all of them, some of the more popular varieties are as follows:

Black beans or turtle soup beans are used in thick soups and in Oriental and Mediterranean dishes.

Black-eyed peas, also called black-eyed beans or "cow peas," are small, oval-shaped, and creamish white with a black spot on one side. They are used primarily as a main dish vegetable. Black-eyed peas are beans. There is no difference in the product. but different names are used in some regions of the country.

Garbanzo beans are known as "chick-peas." These beans are nut flavored and are commonly pickled in vinegar and oil for salads. They can also be used as a main-dish vegetable in the unpickled form. Similar beans are cranberry and yellow-eyed beans.

Great northern beans are larger than pea beans. These beans are used in soups, salads, casserole dishes, and homebaked beans.

Kidney beans are large and have a red color and kidney shape. They are popular for chili con carne and add zest to salads and many Mexican dishes.

Lima beans are not widely known as dry beans. Lima beans make an excellent main-dish vegetable and can be used in casseroles. They are broad and flat. Lima beans come in different sizes, but the size does not affect the quality.

Recalling Facts

1. The pealike bean that inspired the use of "carat" came from
   □ a. Africa.
   □ b. Asia.
   □ c. Europe.

2. Voting was done with beans during the age of the
   □ a. Babylonians.
   □ b. Greeks.
   □ c. Romans.

3. Bean soup is served daily in government dining rooms in
   □ a. Boston.
   □ b. Memphis.
   □ c. Washington, D.C.

4. Beans are processed through the use of
   □ a. electric eyes.
   □ b. pneumatic tubes.
   □ c. magnetic sensors.

5. Black beans are also known as
   □ a. chick-peas.
   □ b. kidney beans.
   □ c. turtle soup beans.

Understanding the Passage

6. Black-eyed peas were so-named because they
   □ a. are unusually dark.
   □ b. are blue before they are cooked.
   □ c. have a black spot on one side.

7. Garbanzo beans are commonly served in
   □ a. thick soups.
   □ b. salads.
   □ c. casseroles.

8. Kidney beans are used most often in the
   □ a. spicy dishes of Mexico.
   □ b. tangy dishes of the Mediterranean region.
   □ c. aromatic dishes of the Orient.

9. The author implies that great northern beans are
   □ a. preferred by ethnic groups in the United States.
   □ b. the most versatile of the bean varieties.
   □ c. often confused with black beans.

10. The reader can conclude that most beans
   □ a. have the same flavor.
   □ b. can be used as main-dish vegetables.
   □ c. grow in warm climates.

50 An Effective Diet

If you intend to start a reducing program, it is wise to check first with your doctor. She can tell if you are in good physical shape for reducing. If you are, she can tell you how much weight to lose and the number of calories to include in your daily diet. She can tell you if exercise or other physical activity is needed.

Plan meals around familiar foods. The only effective diet is the one that is followed daily. For this reason, it is wise to plan meals around foods that are satisfying and are part of the family's way of eating.

When you have reached the right weight, simple additions can be made to the diet so that you can keep your weight.

It is important to create patterns of eating that can be followed when proper weight is attained. Strange and unusual foods and food combinations may seem like a great solution to the dieter's problem, but they are nearly always poor choices as regular food. As a result, the dieter soon may become unhappy and go back to the old food habits that caused the weight gain.

When you plan meals, follow a reliable food plan to be sure of getting the nutritionally important kinds of food. Many reducing diets that include only a few foods are low in needed vitamins and minerals. Such diets should not be followed for any length of time.

Choose low-calorie foods. Avoid such items as added fats, gravies, sauces, fried foods, fatty meats, sweets, pastries, cookies, cakes, alcoholic and soft drinks, and cream.

Season foods with spices, herbs, vinegars, or tart fruit juices to give variety and add interest.

Learn to like cereal or fruit with little or no added sugar. Choose coffee and tea with little or no sugar and cream.

Budget your calories to take care of special occasions, such as holiday meals and parties. Save on calories from other meals to allow extra calories for these.

Snacks, too, can be part of your diet if you plan for them. For example, a piece of fruit or a crisp vegetable, milk, or a simple dessert saved from mealtime can be eaten between meals.

Keep busy so you will not be tempted to eat foods that are not included in your planned meals.

Take advantage of daily chances to increase activities. For instance, walk, rather than ride, whenever possible.

Recalling Facts

1. Before starting a diet, a person should
   - ☐ a. weigh himself.
   - ☐ b. increase exercise.
   - ☐ c. see a doctor.

2. Meals should be planned around foods that are
   - ☐ a. familiar.
   - ☐ b. exotic.
   - ☐ c. tasty.

3. The author advises a person on a diet to avoid
   - ☐ a. alcohol.
   - ☐ b. lean meat.
   - ☐ c. seafood.

4. For the person on a diet, spices, herbs, and vinegars
   - ☐ a. add weight.
   - ☐ b. cause indigestion.
   - ☐ c. give variety.

5. The only effective diet is the one that is
   - ☐ a. totally salt-free.
   - ☐ b. faithfully followed.
   - ☐ c. immediately effective.

Understanding the Passage

6. The author suggests that a person on a diet should
   - ☐ a. eat basically what other members of the family eat.
   - ☐ b. restrict intake of large quantities of water.
   - ☐ c. develop a liking for high protein foods.

7. The author warns that many diets
   - ☐ a. are too expensive for most people to follow.
   - ☐ b. ignore essential nutrition.
   - ☐ c. appeal to the person who does not need to lose weight.

8. The author implies that most people gain weight because of
   - ☐ a. inadequate exercise.
   - ☐ b. poor eating habits.
   - ☐ c. indifference to one's own appearance.

9. Dieting, as recommended in this article, allows
   - ☐ a. birthday parties and holiday meals.
   - ☐ b. eating candy between meals.
   - ☐ c. large helpings at each meal.

10. This article leads the reader to believe that
    - ☐ a. calorie requirements are different for each person.
    - ☐ b. most doctors do not approve of dieting.
    - ☐ c. losing weight is a very difficult process.

Answer Key

Progress Graph

Pacing Graph

Answer Key

1	1. b	2. c	3. b	4. c	5. c	6. c	7. a	8. a	9. b	10. a
2	1. a	2. c	3. a	4. c	5. c	6. c	7. c	8. a	9. c	10. b
3	1. a	2. c	3. c	4. a	5. c	6. c	7. c	8. b	9. c	10. a
4	1. c	2. b	3. a	4. b	5. c	6. c	7. a	8. c	9. c	10. c
5	1. c	2. a	3. c	4. a	5. b	6. c	7. b	8. a	9. a	10. b
6	1. c	2. b	3. b	4. c	5. c	6. a	7. b	8. c	9. b	10. a
7	1. c	2. b	3. a	4. b	5. c	6. a	7. b	8. b	9. a	10. b
8	1. b	2. b	3. a	4. c	5. b	6. a	7. c	8. b	9. b	10. c
9	1. c	2. c	3. b	4. a	5. b	6. c	7. b	8. b	9. a	10. c
10	1. b	2. c	3. a	4. b	5. c	6. a	7. c	8. a	9. a	10. c
11	1. a	2. c	3. b	4. c	5. c	6. b	7. c	8. c	9. c	10. a
12	1. c	2. b	3. a	4. c	5. b	6. c	7. a	8. c	9. c	10. b
13	1. b	2. a	3. b	4. c	5. a	6. a	7. c	8. c	9. a	10. c
14	1. c	2. c	3. a	4. a	5. a	6. a	7. a	8. a	9. c	10. a
15	1. a	2. c	3. c	4. b	5. a	6. c	7. a	8. b	9. a	10. c
16	1. b	2. b	3. c	4. b	5. a	6. b	7. c	8. c	9. a	10. c
17	1. b	2. c	3. c	4. c	5. a	6. c	7. a	8. c	9. b	10. a
18	1. a	2. c	3. b	4. c	5. c	6. c	7. c	8. c	9. c	10. b
19	1. c	2. c	3. c	4. a	5. a	6. b	7. a	8. c	9. b	10. a
20	1. c	2. b	3. b	4. a	5. c	6. a	7. c	8. b	9. b	10. a
21	1. a	2. b	3. c	4. c	5. a	6. b	7. c	8. c	9. b	10. b
22	1. a	2. a	3. b	4. c	5. b	6. c	7. c	8. b	9. a	10. a
23	1. a	2. a	3. c	4. b	5. a	6. b	7. a	8. c	9. a	10. b
24	1. c	2. c	3. b	4. c	5. b	6. b	7. c	8. c	9. b	10. c
25	1. c	2. b	3. a	4. b	5. c	6. a	7. c	8. a	9. c	10. c

26	1. c	2. c	3. c	4. b	5. a	6. c	7. c	8. a	9. c	10. b
27	1. c	2. c	3. b	4. b	5. a	6. b	7. c	8. c	9. a	10. c
28	1. b	2. b	3. c	4. a	5. b	6. b	7. a	8. a	9. b	10. b
29	1. c	2. b	3. c	4. a	5. c	6. c	7. b	8. a	9. b	10. c
30	1. b	2. c	3. c	4. b	5. b	6. b	7. a	8. a	9. b	10. a
31	1. b	2. c	3. a	4. b	5. c	6. c	7. b	8. c	9. a	10. b
32	1. c	2. b	3. c	4. a	5. b	6. b	7. b	8. b	9. a	10. a
33	1. c	2. a	3. a	4. b	5. a	6. a	7. b	8. b	9. c	10. c
34	1. c	2. b	3. b	4. b	5. b	6. b	7. a	8. c	9. a	10. b
35	1. c	2. c	3. a	4. b	5. b	6. c	7. a	8. c	9. a	10. b
36	1. c	2. a	3. a	4. c	5. b	6. c	7. b	8. b	9. b	10. a
37	1. a	2. b	3. b	4. c	5. a	6. b	7. a	8. b	9. a	10. c
38	1. a	2. a	3. b	4. a	5. b	6. c	7. a	8. a	9. b	10. b
39	1. c	2. a	3. c	4. b	5. a	6. b	7. a	8. b	9. c	10. c
40	1. a	2. c	3. b	4. a	5. c	6. b	7. b	8. a	9. b	10. c
41	1. c	2. b	3. a	4. c	5. c	6. a	7. b	8. b	9. a	10. b
42	1. c	2. a	3. c	4. b	5. b	6. a	7. b	8. c	9. b	10. b
43	1. a	2. b	3. c	4. a	5. a	6. a	7. a	8. a	9. b	10. b
44	1. b	2. c	3. b	4. a	5. b	6. b	7. b	8. a	9. b	10. b
45	1. a	2. b	3. b	4. c	5. a	6. a	7. c	8. c	9. a	10. a
46	1. c	2. b	3. a	4. c	5. b	6. c	7. a	8. a	9. b	10. a
47	1. a	2. b	3. a	4. c	5. a	6. c	7. c	8. a	9. b	10. c
48	1. a	2. c	3. c	4. b	5. b	6. b	7. a	8. c	9. c	10. b
49	1. a	2. c	3. c	4. a	5. c	6. c	7. b	8. a	9. b	10. b
50	1. c	2. a	3. a	4. c	5. b	6. a	7. b	8. b	9. a	10. a

Progress Graph (1–25)

Directions: Write your comprehension score in the box under the selection number. Then put an x on the line above each box to show your reading time and words-per-minute reading rate.

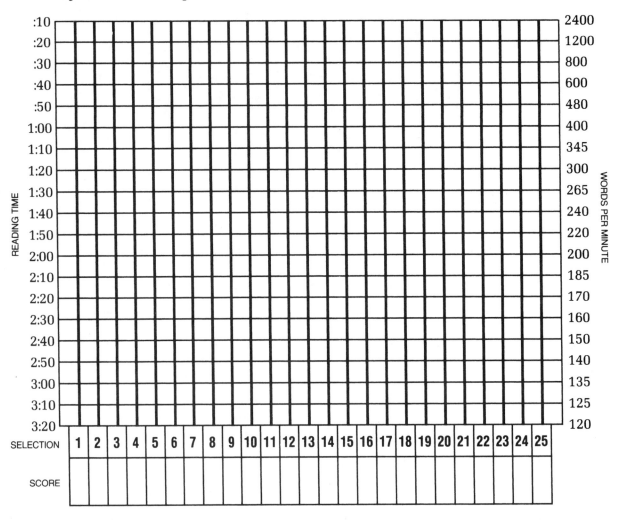

READING TIME		WORDS PER MINUTE
:10		2400
:20		1200
:30		800
:40		600
:50		480
1:00		400
1:10		345
1:20		300
1:30		265
1:40		240
1:50		220
2:00		200
2:10		185
2:20		170
2:30		160
2:40		150
2:50		140
3:00		135
3:10		125
3:20		120

SELECTION	1	2	3	4	5	6	7	8	9	10	11	12	13	14	15	16	17	18	19	20	21	22	23	24	25
SCORE																									

Progress Graph (26–50)

Directions: Write your comprehension score in the box under the selection number. Then put an x on the line above each box to show your reading time and words-per-minute reading rate.

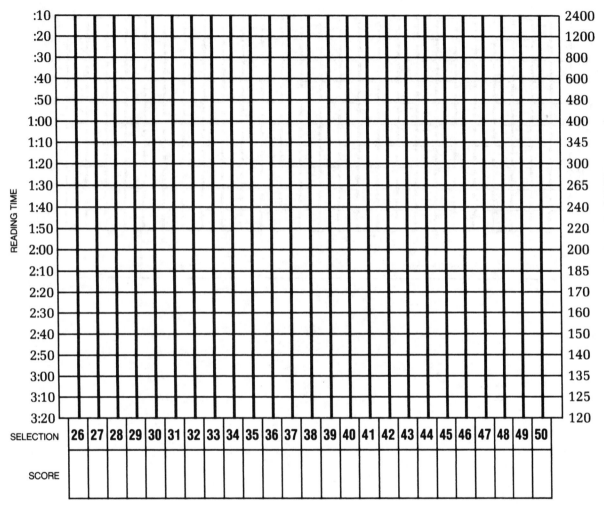

READING TIME		WORDS PER MINUTE
:10		2400
:20		1200
:30		800
:40		600
:50		480
1:00		400
1:10		345
1:20		300
1:30		265
1:40		240
1:50		220
2:00		200
2:10		185
2:20		170
2:30		160
2:40		150
2:50		140
3:00		135
3:10		125
3:20		120

SELECTION: 26 27 28 29 30 31 32 33 34 35 36 37 38 39 40 41 42 43 44 45 46 47 48 49 50

SCORE

Pacing Graph

Directions: In the boxes labeled "Pace" along the bottom of the graph, write your words-per-minute rate. On the vertical line above each box, put an x to indicate your comprehension score.

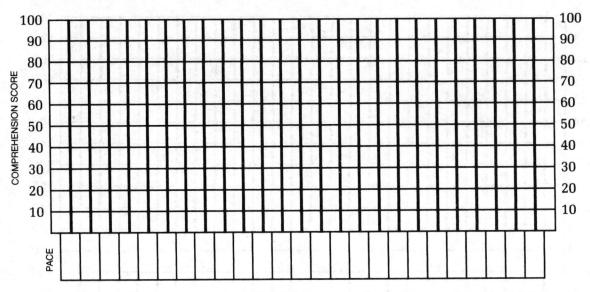